WHAT THE HECK IS CBT?

THE SECRET TO TRAINING AND RESTRUCTURING
NEGATIVE THOUGHTS USING COGNITIVE
BEHAVIORAL THERAPY SKILLS FOR PEOPLE WHO
SUFFER FROM ANXIETY AND DEPRESSION

R.J. MILLER

CONTENTS

FREE SPECIAL GIFT

As a BONUS for purchasing this book,
we would like to give you a
CBT Journal to fastrack your success.

CBT Therapy
JOURNAL

Printable Worksheets

VISIT
**WORKSHEETS.
RJMILLERBOOKS
.COM**

OR...
**GRAB
A COPY
HERE**

SCAN ME

INTRODUCTION

> *"Man is not worried about real problems so much as by his imagined anxieties about real problems."*
>
> — EPICTETUS

You always have arguments with your best friend...

You've just experienced the worst divorce ever...

You broke up with your partner because of your assumptions...

Or perhaps, you've once let go of your dream job because you think you are unqualified for it.

Whatever the case may be, it's normal for everyone to feel sad or gloomy at some point in their life. While it's a fleeting feeling that passes like a storm – the rain clouds clear the sadness. For some people, it's an entirely different story.

For me, when the sadness came, it refused to leave and tagged along wherever I went. Negative thoughts and ruminations were always with me, day and night. Things I used as distractions were no longer working. So, there was no break for me, and life was already a living hell!

With over 6000 thoughts running through the human mind daily, it's not surprising that some thoughts are negative. But why do you give your brain so much work and freedom to accumulate thousands of thoughts? The brain is a mighty powerful organ that becomes incredibly smart when combined with different body systems. However, wires can easily get crossed with a complex organ like the brain, and we end up assuming that the brain knows what it's doing.

Much like when it comes to our problems – the brain will first worry about any problem before there is a chance to create a solution. This typically leads to stress and anxiety way before the potential problem arrives.

So now, let me ask you, what are your biggest fears? Do you have worries that are overwhelming your thought process? Are you worried that your state of mind is blocking you from reaching your goals? Do you find yourself barely coping with a normal life, and when you add criticism from friends, family, or colleagues, bad relationships, burnout, and possibly suicidal thoughts, you can't see a way out of the rut you're in?

All of these questions represent the problems we face in our daily lives. I said "We" because you aren't alone. So many of us have faced similar issues at some point in our lives and are quick to give up the fight and succumb to the effects of ruminating thoughts.

If you are reading this book, you are probably like my old self, who has struggled with negative thoughts. Back then, I was hopeless, and happiness was far away. It was difficult for me to maintain relationships with family members, friends, and colleagues. My symptoms felt like I was being knocked down over and over again. As a result, I lost interest in things I normally enjoyed. And I really didn't have much of an appetite anymore.

Whenever I go through a difficult experience or feel distressed about something, it always feels like my thoughts are running out of control. My mind will start racing, and I find myself constantly dwelling on the past and worrying about what is to come. My thoughts can sometimes be so consuming that it is almost impossible to focus on anything else. Being loving to friends and family, empathic to colleagues, productive at work, or even carrying on a simple conversation seemed impossible. The thoughts were so persistent that nothing could distract me from them... nothing could hold my attention or even try slowing down my thoughts to give me a moment of peace.

My family called me paranoid and irrational and felt I was exaggerating my feelings and problems. Looking back now, I can't even blame them for thinking that way because they had little or no understanding of different mental health conditions.

Since it's natural to want unwanted thoughts to disappear from my head, I always try to push them aside and set myself free from them altogether. But the more I try to fight off unwanted negative thoughts, the stronger they become and take hold of me.

Of course, I tried different types of self-help, including reading books and listening to podcasts, but I didn't get the results I had hoped for. I knew some kind of therapy would be beneficial, but I wasn't comfortable talking to others about my situation. Then, during my research, I came across CBT, which eventually changed my life. CBT has become a healthy part of my daily routine for four years now.

Just like it changed mine and the lives of celebrities like John Green and Ellie Goulding, I believe CBT can change your life too. With CBT, I could retrain my brain, conquer ruminations and negative thoughts, and regain control of my life. Yes! I combatted my PTSD with CBT. But first, you need to understand what CBT entails and how it can help you reconstruct negative thought patterns and overcome physical and mental health conditions such as anxiety, depression, addiction, PTSD, chronic pain, panic attacks, and Attention-deficit/hyperactivity disorder(ADHD).

CBT is an evidence-based treatment that taught me how negative thoughts teamed up with my intense emotions, shutting me down to depress me further. As I recognized the irrational thoughts, I could change them into positive statements. For example, instead of thinking my boss hates me because she assigns the most challenging tasks to me, why don't I see it as she assigns those tasks to me because she believes in me and knows I can handle them?

This was me fighting so hard and taking a fearless inventory of myself over time. By taking this approach, I could confidently talk to my boss and ask for a raise and possibly the promotion I was due for. Little by little, I realized the unproductive thought patterns I was creating. Even though I didn't feel like my symptoms would get better at times, I didn't stop practicing my CBT techniques and skills; I kept going.

This book doesn't promise a magical cure but provides practical strategies to manage symptoms that limit you and empower you to change. It will take you through a journey that guarantees favorable results.

First, we'll start from the foundation by introducing you to the philosophy behind CBT. Then, we'll explore the human thought processes and consequences that follow. We'll also discuss the different health conditions you can treat with CBT and how to apply the strategies to rewire your brain and become more positive. Whether you are in therapy or not, you can gain a lot from this book.

Despite being short-term, CBT is a goal-oriented approach with significant long-term effects and can be done independently. The results can be instant, making it difficult or frustrating for you to see it to the end. You need a support system to ensure you practice for weeks to gain the full benefits. With your collaboration, your negative thoughts and feelings will pass like a dark cloud on a sunny day.

Depression, anxiety, and other problems you may face don't have to last a lifetime. CBT can help you work through your challenges quickly. Since your thoughts, feelings, and behaviors are connected, you can change your life entirely by changing your thoughts. Do you remember the happiness and enthusiasm you felt when you were younger? It will return once again.

Now, are you ready to kick-start your journey for transformative change with your mental health? Join me in the first chapter as I'll introduce the philosophy behind CBT.

THE PHILOSOPHY BEHIND COGNITIVE BEHAVIORAL THERAPY

One in every five people experiences a mental health issue at least once yearly, with anxiety and depression topping the list. Many of us are already familiar with what it means to be sad or excessively worried about something. However, for some, the feelings can be overwhelming and bigger than they can manage. This is where getting help comes in.

Cognitive behavioral therapy (CBT) principles are of great use to those interested in the concept of positive psychology. This psychological intervention has proven effective in treating patients with anxiety, depression, and other psychological conditions.

Becoming increasingly mindful of one's thoughts and learning to interrupt negative thoughts can help you develop a healthier and more positive outlook and a deeper understanding of your power over your behavior. This is the basis of CBT! By seeking to understand your cognition and its link to behavior more in-depth, you can change how you think, and by effect, your life.

Like any relatively new concept, CBT comes with misconceptions – the most prominent being that CBT is all about learning to be positive. In other words, you transform a negative thought into a positive one. While this may appear true to an extent, it doesn't tell the whole story about this popular psychotherapeutic treatment. This misconception is inaccurate, potentially harmful, and a far cry from the truth.

To burst the unfounded myths and misconceptions about CBT and separate what's true from what isn't, let's begin by discussing what CBT is and a brief history of the intervention.

WHAT IS CBT?

CBT is a talk therapy intervention focusing on the relationship between one's thoughts, emotions, and behaviors. It deals with identifying and challenging negative thoughts and self-defeating beliefs. As these are identified, you can now form new thinking patterns, improving your feelings and behaviors.

This type of talk therapy can be described as a combination of psychotherapy and behavioral therapy. Psychotherapy deals with the personal meaning of thinking patterns developed in childhood, whereas behavioral therapy focuses on the intimate relationship between thoughts, behavior, and personal problems.

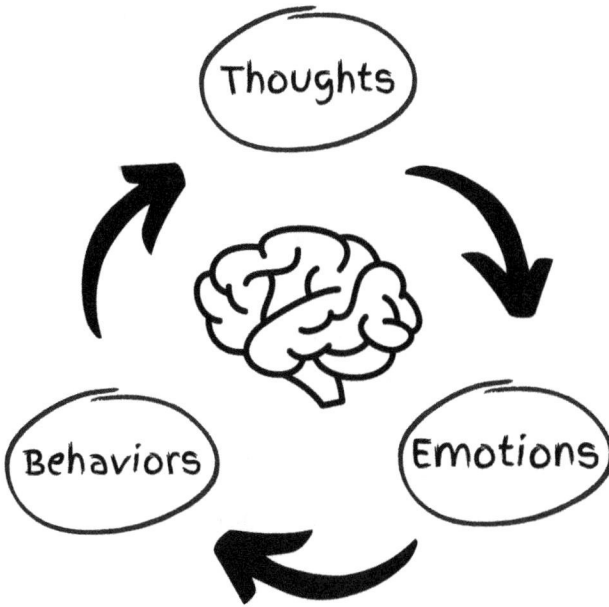

The origins of CBT go back to two different psychology schools: Behaviorism and Cognitive therapy. There has been the behavioral treatment for psychological disorders since the 1900s. Pavlov, Skinner, and Watson were key proponents of behavioral treatments.

Albert Ellis and Aaron T. Beck were two key proponents of cognitive therapy. In the 1950s, Ellis developed Rational Emotive Behavior Therapy (REBT) with the goal of helping patients identify irrational thought patterns. The idea is that emotional distress arises from thoughts. Therefore, by identifying irrational thoughts, you can challenge the pattern and shift to a more rational thought pattern.

Cognitive therapy became popular as a standalone therapy in the 1960s with the discovery of Aaron T. Beck. He noticed a pattern in his depressed patients. He found that they all negatively perceived themselves, the world, and the future. In addition, they also experienced a stream of spontaneous negative thoughts. With his findings, Beck began to form theories on alternate ways of examining and treating depression.

Beck's theory of cognitive distortions and Ellis' theory of irrational thinking offered a better approach to understanding psychological problems individually. So Beck began to use his approach to help clients reevaluate their thoughts. And in doing so, these clients found long-lasting change and became more resilient in handling life's daily functions.

CBT practice grew in the mid-1970s, particularly in treating high-functioning patients. It became stronger through trial and error, further behavioral therapy advancements, and a much-improved understanding of emotional control.

Beck found that there was a critical link between thoughts and feelings. So he came up with the term "automatic thoughts" to describe thoughts that spontaneously popped up in people's heads uninvited.

He also discovered that even though his patients weren't always conscious of these thoughts in their heads, they could learn to identify them. Beck found that people could achieve positive, long-lasting change simply by uncovering these automatic thoughts and challenging them. In essence, Cognitive Therapy helps people to recognize unhelpful thoughts and challenge them. This then makes it possible to find alternatives and open up choices.

Behavioral therapy was used to treat anxiety and phobias effectively. Still, it wasn't until it was combined with cognitive therapy that psychologists could use CBT to treat a wider range of psychological disorders and conditions.

CBT is constantly evaluating its techniques. The result of this is a comprehensive body of research about the effectiveness of this therapy method in treating a wide range of psychological issues. It's necessary to emphasize that CBT techniques have advanced based on research and clinical practice. It is one of the psychological approaches supported with ample evidence that its techniques can actually effect change. In this sense, CBT is different from many types of psychological treatment.

The following are the core principles of CBT:

- Psychological issues are due, in part, to faulty and self-defeating ways of thinking.
- Psychological issues are due, in part, to acquire patterns of self-destructive behavior.
- Individuals suffering from psychological problems can learn to cope with them in better ways, thus relieving symptoms and becoming more functional and effective in daily life.

CBT treatment strategies usually try to change behavioral patterns. They might include:

- Learning to confront one's fears instead of avoiding them.

- Role-playing to learn how to handle potentially problematic interactions.
- Calming one's mind and relaxing one's body in distressing situations.

Not all types of CBT use these strategies. In many cases, the psychologist and client work collaboratively to understand the underlying problem and develop an intervention specific to the client's needs.

CBT emphasizes the importance of helping people be their own therapists, which is considered the most effective approach. Treatment focuses on what's happening in the client's current life rather than past experiences that led to the present difficulties.

Of course, some information about one's past is required. Still, the therapy focuses primarily on getting through the present and going forward in time to come up with better ways of handling life's difficulties.

CBT's approach to treating psychological disorders has pros and cons. Like all therapies, there's a risk of negative feelings returning. Here's a list of advantages CBT offers:

- Unlike other talk therapies, CBT treatments can be completed in a relatively short time frame.
- It can help treat certain mental disorders where medication isn't improving symptoms.
- CBT focuses on modifying thoughts and behavior to change how you feel.

- The strategies are practical and helpful. They can help you learn to cope with future stress.
- CBT is practicable in different formats, including online, in-person, or workbooks.
- It can improve a person's emotional processing skills.

Here's a list of things that one may consider cons of CBT:

- CBT requires you to commit to the process every step of the way. It's not a magic wand that will make your problems go away. You have to put in the work,
- Even if your needs are met through CBT, your environment (interactions, family) can counteract the impact.
- CBT is usually more difficult for individuals with severe mental health disorders.
- Some CBT strategies use exposure to address anxiety sources, which can be uncomfortable.
- Putting in the work in your life will take time, commitment, and patience.

Why Don't We Just Become More Positive?

We said earlier that there are many misconceptions about CBT – the biggest being that CBT is all about having people think positively. Unfortunately, this misconception birthed the erroneous assumption that CBT trains clients to ignore negative happenings in their lives to preserve their experience of positive emotions.

Unsurprisingly, those with this view tend to perceive CBT negatively and may even avoid working with CBT practitioners. In reality, the primary goal of CBT is to help you achieve balanced thinking. Balanced thinking involves evaluating all the information and context in a situation that contributes to your emotional state. This means you must learn to process both positive and negative information effectively. You cannot simply disregard the negative and focus solely on the positive.

Contrary to popular belief, CBT doesn't advocate disregarding negative information or replacing negative information with a positive one. There are many reasons why it's crucial to process both negative and positive information. First, negative emotions exist for a reason – to warn you about a need for change. People often experience stressful life events and challenges, which should be addressed. Disregarding such negative experiences is illogical because it won't help you feel better.

By this same token, CBT helps you to evaluate the positive information and context in a situation. Contrary to belief, the positive information you're encouraged to consider is one supported by evidence, not information based on "positive affirmations," which isn't supported by facts or evidence.

Most people tend to hyper-fixate on the negative when in a distressing situation. This is why CBT encourages us to consider genuine negative and positive information. However, focusing solely on the negative can intensify the degree of distress an individual feels in the situation. Among difficult emotions are anger, frustration, sadness, anxiety, guilt, and embarrassment – to name a few.

In contrast, the intensity of a difficult emotion decreases when you balance your thinking and interpretation of a situation. This approach helps you cope with the emotional aspect of the situation in a better way, which then makes you handle the behavioral aspect more effectively with problem-solving and action.

Adopting a "positive-thoughts-only" attitude makes you vulnerable to the risk of toxic positivity. This over-the-top form of positivity encourages you to invalidate your true feelings. Toxic positivity is the excessive overgeneralization of a happy, upbeat emotional state, no matter the situation. It contributes to the minimization or blatant denial of an authentic emotional experience.

Unfortunately, suppressing negative emotions and masking them with an outward appearance of positivity can only intensify the feelings, increasing discomfort. Like anything done excessively, positivity becomes toxic when it's used to silence the authentic human experience. By dismissing or disallowing the experience of certain emotions, we fall into a perpetual state of denial and repressed feelings.

The reality is that humans are not perfect. Emotions like anger, jealousy, sadness, and greed, as undesirable as they are, make us who we are. So, pretending that it's "positive vibes always" denies the validity of your genuine experience as a human being.

Balanced thinking is important because focusing solely on the positives of a situation prevents you from identifying and addressing negative events in your life, likely contributing to your emotional distress.

Also, focusing solely on the negative gives you a skewed view of the situation, further intensifying your distress. That makes it more difficult to address stressful events and problems in your life.

While it is a misconception that CBT focuses on positivity only, there are times when it's best to process only positive information.

The bottom line is that CBT encourages us to take a balanced approach to critically think and interpret information – a balance of negatives and positives. That is the only practical way to enhance your experience and enjoyment of life.

CBT Compared With Other Forms of Therapy

Before we talk about the difference between CBT and other therapy approaches, it's important to understand the approaches themselves and what they entail. Psychotherapy offers a roadmap for psychologists to understand their client's problems and develop effective solutions. To do this, psychotherapists take five approaches:

- **Psychoanalysis therapy:** This category of psychotherapy focuses on changing unhelpful behaviors, thoughts, and feelings by unraveling the unconscious meanings and motivations behind them. Therapies that use this approach involve a collaborative partnership between therapist and client. As a result, the client (patient) discovers more about themselves as they explore their interactions with the therapist.

- **Behavior therapy:** This psychotherapy approach focuses on the role of learning in developing normal and abnormal behaviors. It is characterized by concepts such as classical conditioning (associative learning), desensitizing, and operant conditioning. With classical conditioning, a therapist could help a patient develop a specific behavior by associating it with something else. For example, Ivan Pavlov trained his famous dogs to drool at the sound of their dinner bell by associating the sound with food. On the other hand, desensitizing involves repeatedly exposing a client to the source of their anxiety. Meanwhile, operant conditioning uses reward and punishment to shape behavior.

- **Cognitive therapy:** As you already know, cognitive therapy focuses on thought (what you think) rather than behavior (what you believe). Building on the work of Aaron T. Beck, cognitive therapists believe dysfunctional thinking causes dysfunctional feelings and behavior. So, by changing your thoughts, you can change how you feel and what you do.

- **Humanistic therapy:** This approach to psychotherapy concerns people's capacity to make rational decisions (choices) and reach their maximum potential. It also focuses on respect and concern for other people.

- **Integrative (holistic) therapy:** Many therapists don't restrict themselves to any one category of psychotherapy. Instead, they combine techniques from different approaches and tailor their intervention to individual clients' needs.

The core difference between CBT and these other approaches is that it is effective for a wider range of conditions.

CBT encompasses four approaches and a broad range of techniques to address one's thoughts, emotions, and behaviors. The practice can range from structured therapy to self-help. Your specific approach will depend on the issue (s) being addressed. Regardless, four therapeutic approaches incorporate CBT.

Dialectical Behavior Therapy (DBT)

Dialectical behavioral therapy is an evidence-based CBT approach that employs problem-solving strategies and teaches clients to find acceptance. In addition, it is used to address distressing thoughts and behavior by incorporating strategies such as mindfulness and emotional regulation.

DBT is effective in treating emotional dysregulation and several mental health disorders. However, clients who benefit from this approach tend to view things from a "black-and-white lens." They regard situations as this or the other, which makes it difficult to see a gray area or find a middle ground.

This type of CBT can potentially help anyone who lacks emotional coping skills and always finds themselves in one crisis or another. In addition, it can potentially allow you to acquire the skills needed to cope with distressing emotions effectively.

DBT can be used to treat anyone with Bipolar Disorder, Borderline Personality Disorder, ADHD, Post Traumatic Stress Disorder, and Eating disorders.

Mindfulness-Based Cognitive Therapy (MBCT)

Mindfulness-based cognitive therapy combines CBT with mindfulness meditation to help cultivate a present-oriented and non-judgmental attitude toward your experiences. It can effectively handle anxiety, depression, and bipolar disorder.

Acceptance and Commitment Therapy (ACT)

Some argue that ACT is purely a behavioral therapy, but it can be classified as a form of CBT. It is a behavior-oriented approach that emphasizes the use of positive reinforcement and counter-conditioning to change how a person responds to their internal experiences.

Internal experiences include:

- Thoughts
- Emotions
- Impulses
- Physical feelings

Acceptance and commitment therapy can help you learn to stop avoiding, denying, and fighting with your inner feelings. With this approach, you learn that certain feelings are appropriate emotional responses to the situations that trigger them. It teaches you to recognize and accept them.

Once you understand that, it becomes easy to accept the challenges and issues that life throws at you. Acceptance is the foundation for making behavioral changes that ultimately improve your life.

ACT can teach you to cope effectively with the following:

- Depression
- Chronic pain
- Workplace stress
- Substance abuse and addiction
- Obsessive-compulsive disorder
- Test-based anxiety

Rational emotive Behavior therapy (REBT)

REBT is a therapy approach that focuses on helping clients to identify irrational beliefs, including negative thoughts and self-defeating feelings. This active-oriented approach will teach you to challenge irrational beliefs until you can eventually recognize and change your unhelpful thought patterns. The ultimate goal is to teach you to swap negative beliefs for healthier, more productive ones.

This type of CBT can be used to help clients struggling with:

- Anxiety
- Depression
- Guilt
- Anger issues
- Procrastination

- Disordered eating
- Aggression

Once again, the type (s) of CBT treatments you'll receive depends on which areas of your life you want to improve with this effective 'talking' therapy.

WHAT IS CBT USED FOR?

Over the past few decades, CBT has been increasingly adopted over other treatment therapies as psychology shifted toward evidence-based practice. Psychology research has established CBT as the most effective therapy for various mental health conditions.

This therapy approach is almost always more effective in treating many mental health issues than medication or traditional talk therapy. Studies have also shown that CBT has the lowest relapse rate of all psychological treatments.

CBT can be used to treat the following range of conditions successfully:

- Anxiety
- Depression
- Phobias
- Panic Disorder
- Obsessive Compulsive Disorder
- Eating disorders
- Addictions
- Bipolar Disorder

- Schizophrenia
- Psychosis
- Anger issues
- Chronic fatigue syndrome
- Irritable bowel syndrome
- Fibromyalgia
- Personality disorders
- Substance misuse

CBT can be a short-term intervention to help you learn to analyze thoughts and beliefs. In addition to these mental health conditions, CBT can also help people cope with the following:

- Chronic pain
- Insomnia
- Serious health issues, such as cancer
- Divorce or painful break-ups
- Grief or loss
- Trauma
- Low self-esteem
- Stress management
- Relationship problems

The fact that CBT is the best treatment available for the afore-mentioned mental health conditions is supported by it being one of the most researched therapy approaches.

Here's some research that proves that CBT is indeed effective for this range of mental health conditions.

- A 2018 review involving 41 studies that looked at the use of CBT in treating anxiety disorders, OCD, and PTSD discovered that CBT could help improve the symptoms of all these conditions. In addition, it was found to be the most effective approach for anxiety, stress, and OCD.
- A 2018 research studying CBT for anxiety found that the therapy produced good long-term results. However, the study focused on young people, and more than half of the participants no longer met the criteria for anxiety two years after the intervention.
- A 2018 study involving 104 participants found evidence that CBT can improve cognitive function in people with PTSD and major depression.
- Recent research from 2020 and 2021 finds that virtual and internet-based CBT practice is promising for effective treatment.
- Studies from 2010 found CBT to be effective in treating substance misuse. The National Institute on Drug Abuse reports that CBT can be used to help cope with addiction and prevent relapse after treatment.

Numerous ongoing research studies are still looking into the efficacy of CBT in treating even more mental health conditions.

IS CBT FOR EVERYONE?

CBT may be more effective than medication or traditional talk therapy in treating many mental health problems, but that doesn't make it suitable for everyone. Moreover, not everyone will succeed with CBT due to a couple of factors we're about to discuss.

CBT has been proven to help adults, teens, and kids. However, it is one form of therapy that emphasizes structure. If you struggle with structure, you may find it harder to use CBT to address your issues.

Additionally, it requires you to take an active role in the therapy process. While your therapist can help break down your thoughts and feelings so you can examine them more closely, you'll most likely end each session with some type of homework that teaches coping skills you're expected to apply in different aspects of your life.

Also, CBT requires you to closely examine your thoughts and feelings, which can be incredibly hard for some people. The process takes time, commitment, and dedication. You must be willing to do the work required for change to happen. Some people may find this hard or outright impossible.

The techniques involve lots of homework you must be willing to get done if you don't want to risk impeding your progress or success. Therefore, commitment and dedication are crucial for a successful CBT treatment.

One thing about CBT is that it tends to look a lot different for clients, depending on the mental health condition they are treating. For example, someone treated for bipolar disorder or schizophrenia will have an entirely different experience than someone using CBT to address anxiety or panic disorder.

In many cases, CBT emphasizes the therapy process over the relationship between therapist and client. However, suppose you would like to build an emotional rapport with your therapist. In that case, this approach may not deliver in some cases.

As stated previously, CBT uses a shorter treatment time frame than other treatment methods. In some cases, it is limited to just 6-12 sessions. Therefore, if you want a therapy that goes in-depth into your issues and covers the bases, this one may not suit you.

It's important to acknowledge and accept the reality that CBT may not work for you. Otherwise, you'll end up blaming yourself or the therapist when it doesn't solve your issues. You might think, "Oh, there must be nothing that can help me if even CBT fails. I am a real lost cause." That is far from the truth.

If you've tried CBT for a while and didn't notice any improvement in your life, you might need to consider a different type of intervention.

There are various approaches to psychotherapy. For example, if you're doing CBT with a therapist rather than by yourself, you might ask them for other interventions you can do along with or combined with CBT.

Or, you might check the self-help section on Amazon or a local bookstore and find workbooks that offer a different therapeutic approach to your problems. For example, if your problem is connected to relationships, you might find family or couples therapy more effective.

Sometimes, what you need to do for CBT to work is to increase your "dosage." Building momentum is difficult if you aren't working hard enough between sessions, as this therapy boils down to commitment and consistency to achieve your end goal.

In many cases, all it takes to unlock the effectiveness of CBT is to create more time between sessions to practice the skills you learn. Then, reflect on your current therapy "dosage" and see if you need to adjust it.

Remember, there is solid research supporting the use of CBT in helping a wide variety of people with an even wider variety of mental health symptoms. The approach is an excellent place to start if you're entering therapy, but that doesn't make it a cure-all. If CBT doesn't help you or isn't effective for all of your symptoms, you have numerous options.

By now, you should be motivated by everything you've learned about CBT. It shows that there is hope ahead of the road. Yes, you might feel slightly abashed by the idea of having to do plenty of homework during this journey, but don't let that demotivate you. If you commit to your homework as much as you did in high school, you'll find success with CBT.

In the next chapter, we will discuss how the brain functions in relation to thoughts and the ease with which it can be confused or distorted.

Chapter One Highlights

- CBT is an established treatment for chronic stress, anxiety, depression, pain, and other mental health conditions. Compared to other therapy approaches, it is the best-studied psychotherapy for treating psychological issues relating to cognition and behavior.
- CBT techniques can change how you feel and behave by addressing faulty or self-destructive thoughts and replacing them with positive ones. As a result, you can learn to cope with your psychological problems in healthier ways by changing how you view and respond to them.
- The key to overcoming psychological issues is to adopt a balanced view of positive and negative information rather than focusing on positivity alone. Negative emotions exist to help you navigate life's many challenges, so you cannot completely disregard or suppress them.
- You are not perfect; nobody is. It's normal and acceptable to experience unpleasant emotions because they make you who you are. Don't deny or repress the validity of your "negative" emotions because that impairs your outlook on life and makes it difficult to address stressors and challenges in life.
- CBT is more effective than traditional therapies and medications, but it may not be suitable for you. If you want to be successful with this approach, you must be willing to take an active role in the treatment process.

THE THOUGHT PROCESS AND CONSEQUENCES

For an organ roughly three (3) pounds in size, you'll agree with me that the brain has extensive responsibilities – from body movement, to your senses, organs, speech, and the regulation of the entire body system. The brain is also responsible for cognitive processes, i.e., thoughts and emotions. Like any part of your body, your cognition won't function as it should if you don't take good care of the brain.

Your brain processes nearly 80 000 thoughts daily. But have you ever wondered where these come from? Or what are they made of? And if you can measure them? Do you think while doing something else, or is this part of the brain on auto-pilot? In other words, do we form thoughts automatically?

The big question should be, have you ever thought about your thoughts? Oops... now you're thinking about them.

Okay, the first thing I aim to help you understand in this chapter is how thoughts form. And I'll do that by explaining how the brain creates a neural pathway for thought processes. Heads up! This chapter might seem a bit more technical since we'll be discussing the thought processes which relate to the brain. However, I will ensure I make it as simple as possible.

WHERE DO OUR THOUGHTS STEM FROM?

What were your assumptions when you started reading this book? You probably thought, "Alright, it's time to see what there is to know about CBT" or something similar. But first, let's deconstruct this thought to determine exactly what it is.

The first step to understanding where thoughts come from is determining what a thought is. You would probably define a thought as "something I tell myself."

Phew, that's quite something. And, depending on who you pose the question ("what is a thought?)", you'll get different answers.

Of course, from a psychological perspective, we'll focus on the reductionist theory that describes thoughts as *"physical entities that chemical changes in the brain can explain."*

Although the science of neuron communication is well-studied, scientists have yet to accurately define the complexity of cognitive processes.

The brain contains approximately 100 billion cells called neurons. These neurons produce what you may know as neurotransmitters – a bunch of chemicals that create electrical signals in the neurons, allowing them to communicate with one another.

Thoughts are electrochemical reactions that take place in the brain. When neurons release neurotransmitters, they generate these electrical impulses, which travel like waves to thousands of neighboring neurons, leading to thought formation. But that's just a single thought formation, right? If so, how do thought patterns then form?

One theory is that thoughts form when neurons fire. External stimuli create repeated neuron firing, reinforcing the circuitry and producing a thought pattern. If you find yourself in the same situation twice, your neurons will fire similarly, reinforcing them. As noted, that's why we react to similar situations the same way, since the neurons responsible for our response fire again and again.

Often, we repeat certain actions (driving, cooking, or singing a favorite song), which activate the same neurons until they become familiar to us. This creates a reinforced circuit related to these activities. The same applies to situations that trigger a reaction in us.

This is fascinating, as it means you can shift from a negative thought pattern to a positive one or change a behavior. Now, note that tracking a particular harmful thought will trigger a change in how neurons fire, essentially leading to the formation of a new thought process.

Thoughts are your perceptions, beliefs, and ideas about your environment. It is the lens by which you see your entire existence. In addition, they are a filter for how you perceive the world. We're all familiar with the word "attitude," which often has a negative connotation. A long-lasting thought transforms into an attitude, whether positive or negative.

The complexity of the brain's chemical processes of thought formation is why our thoughts are so hard to track. A single neuron firing can range from 1 to 1000 signals per second. As a result, we tend to underestimate the capacity of our brains. Think about the number of neurotransmitters fired as you read this line. Trust me; it's a lot!

As you're reading this, the letter photons go straight to your retina, from where the light-detecting cells detect them – turning them into electrical signals. The electrical signals are then transported to the nerve cells, which quickly spread to neighboring nerve cells. You don't even realize it, but that electrochemical signal activates billions of neurons in seconds. Incredible, right?

Sometimes, you notice a catchy tune from your favorite artist replaying in your head over and over, and you're constantly humming along. You often don't pay conscious attention when you drive home from work, but you take a right turn anyway. You might even be lost in your thoughts while driving, and you won't make mistakes.

Cognitive neuroscience says that only 5% of our cognitive activities are done consciously. That means 95% of these activities, including thinking, are done subconsciously. In essence, your brain has adapted to making you perform many activities without being constantly aware. Scientists call this "adaptive unconscious."

The "adaptive unconscious" ensures you don't make tedious calculations every time you're driving. And you can be more attentive as you engage in that activity like the first time you tried it. Once you learn something, you don't forget it.

As you might have figured, this is the same as automatic negative thoughts. They are in your subconscious, shaping your behavior and attitude toward life, and you don't even realize it.

In the past, we believed that once neural connections were formed, they remained for good. But today, we know that neurons create synapses, which are like branches. So we use some regularly, thereby strengthening them. Meanwhile, the ones we don't use are eliminated. This is called neuroplasticity.

According to Dr. Celeste Campbell, a neuropsychologist in the Polytrauma Program at the Washington, DC Veterans Administration Medical Center, "From the time the brain begins to develop in utero until the day we die, the connections among our brain cells reorganize in response to our changing needs. This process allows us to learn from and adapt to different experiences."

Every time you learn something new, the brain creates new connections between your nerve cells. Every day, the brain rewires itself to adapt to new experiences and circumstances. That is how remarkable this organ truly is. But you can also stimulate and encourage neuroplasticity without waiting for your brain to do it. In other words, you're capable of changing your brain and the way it thinks.

HOW THOUGHTS, EMOTIONS, AND BEHAVIORS ARE LINKED

Have you ever wondered why you can't stop repeating a particular behavior or why you can't help feeling a specific way no matter how hard you try?

Awareness of your thoughts and feelings is vital for your mental wellness. As humans, we're hardwired to think and feel. However, the range of thoughts and feelings you experience can make it hard to understand how they may affect your life.

Thoughts and feelings have a profound impact on your daily life. They help you make sense of your environment and connect you with the world.

Recognizing that thoughts and feelings are two distinct things is key to processing them. To become better at processing and understanding your thoughts and feelings, know what they are, what they aren't, the relationship between them, and how they differ from each other. Note that it can take time and patience to differentiate between your feelings and thoughts.

You might feel confused if you try to understand thoughts and feelings on your own, partly because of how you refer to them. Many times, we say, "I'm feeling this way," even though it's, in fact, not a feeling.

For example, you might say, "I feel stupid." This isn't a real feeling. The correct statement is, "I think I am stupid," because it's a thought. And you probably have that thought because you feel sad, hurt, or ashamed. Therefore, "I feel sad because I think I am stupid" is more accurate.

Many of us aren't aware of the impact of our thoughts and feelings on behavior. The way you think about a situation affects how you feel about it. Your thoughts and feelings influence your behaviors, choices, and outcomes. Thoughts, emotions, and behavior are interconnected. Your thoughts can trigger certain feelings, which, in turn, can trigger specific behaviors.

To understand the connection between all three, let's define them individually. When you understand that connection, you'll be able to modify your thoughts, emotions, and behavior to improve your mental and emotional wellness – which is the whole point of learning CBT.

Since you already know what thoughts are, let's briefly explain what emotions and behaviors are.

Emotions

These are feelings triggered by your thoughts or experiences – from happiness to sadness, anger, anxiety, fear, surprise, and other feelings. You experience these feelings in varying intensity, usually with associated physiological signs. For instance, when you're anxious, you may feel like there is a pit at the bottom of your stomach. And when you're angry, you may feel tightness in your chest.

Strong emotions can make it difficult to think logically. This is due to the impact of emotions on how you think and make decisions. For example, anger can make you react irrationally and do or say something you would never say in a normal state of mind.

Emotions are universal experiences, and you need to learn to express them. There is no such thing as a "bad" feeling. Every emotion exists because it serves a purpose.

Behaviors

These are the actions you take as a response to your emotions. They are the way you present yourself to others. Your behaviors are an outward expression of how you feel internally. If someone finds communicating their thoughts or feelings hard, you can look to their behaviors for clues.

When you experience a strong emotion, you're prompted to act on it, sometimes without thinking. Unfortunately, this can make you behave in ways you might regret later. For instance, you might yell or scream at someone if you're experiencing an emotion like anger. Or if you're feeling sad, you might withdraw from others or cry alone in your room.

Behavioral changes typically indicate an internal struggle. They are signs that someone may be struggling with a mental health problem. If you want to know whether someone you know finds it hard to discuss their thoughts or feelings, compare their behavior before and after stress. The more significant the difference in their behavior, the greater their internal struggle.

The Connection Explained!

The connection between thoughts, emotions, and behavior is pretty straightforward: your behaviors are directly tied to your feelings, and vice versa. Because of this, you can change your behavior by changing your feelings; and you can change your feelings by changing your behavior.

This is why clinical psychologists say that we can fight depression by actively changing specific behaviors. It's the most direct way to help many people struggling with depression improve their mood.

Also, work on identifying the emotions that trigger certain behaviors. Then, you can learn to manage your behavior by handling your emotions better.

In all of this, you might be wondering where thoughts fit in. Thoughts encompass words, pictures, speech, and even smells. Thoughts in this context refer to different mental activities, such as plans, hopes, wishes, judgments, predictions, and memories.

You don't notice your thoughts most of the time – but they are there in the background, helping you to complete tasks automatically and shaping your decisions. Sometimes, you become aware of these thoughts – for example, when you try to remember something that happened a few years back or learn a new skill.

Thoughts and feelings are intricately linked, as thoughts can evoke strong emotions. For example, if you find your work quite stressful, you might start to experience anxiety anytime you're at work. In turn, the feeling of anxiety could cause you to have automatic negative thoughts (ANTs). Such as thinking you aren't good enough or that you'll lose your job if you can't handle the pressure. Of course, this does nothing but reinforce your negative emotional state, keeping you in a cycle that's hard to break out of.

Another example is if you enjoy swimming or being near water outdoors. The mere thought of going to a pool can evoke feelings of happiness and excitement. In turn, those feelings can prompt you to plan activities that include being around water.

However, if you're afraid of large bodies of water, such as a river or pool, or the thought of swimming scares you, you'll naturally avoid plans that include such activities. Depending on your thoughts, the same experience can evoke different feelings (excitement or anxiety). In this case, there is no right or wrong – you simply have different views of the same situation or experience.

Try the exercise below to know whether automatic thoughts profoundly and immediately impact your feelings and behavior.

Imagine that you're walking home from the theater on a dark Saturday evening. It's quite late, and you're wondering whether you should still have dinner by this time. Your thoughts are interrupted by a quiet, rustling noise a few steps away from you. What is it?

Thought 1 – "It's a stray cat."

What do you feel immediately when this thought pops into your head? How does it affect your emotions? What do you do at that moment?

It's a cat, so you relax and keep walking toward the metro. And you return to thinking about your dinner.

Thought 2 - "It's a mugger."

What do you feel when this thought pops into your head? How does it affect your emotions? What do you do differently at that moment?

This will probably evoke a different feeling and reaction from the first thought. You may tense up in fear or anxiety. Your hands start to sweat, your heartbeat might increase, and your tummy churns.

What do you do? Maybe you increase your steps or look for a place to run or hide. Then, you see a cat come out from your left and instantly relax.

This scenario highlights how a simple thought (not fact) can change your feelings and actions. That is an excellent example of the link between your thoughts, feelings, and behaviors. Aaron T. Beck emphasized the importance of this relationship. He proposed that changing one of the three (thoughts, emotions, and behaviors) would change any of the others.

The essence of CBT is that changing cognition, behavior, or both can change emotion and improve symptoms of specific mental health problems.

While you might be tempted to ignore your thoughts or suppress difficult feelings in order to cope with them, by doing this, you risk making irrational decisions that may lead to unhealthy results.

For example, if someone close does something to hurt you, the secondary emotion you'll experience is most likely anger. But you may try to suppress the anger because it's painful and not in line with what you feel for the person who hurt you.

You may feel conflicted about your anger and, in that case, decide to suppress the feelings rather than cope with the pain. However, pushing those feelings down can trigger more negative feelings, making you feel worse.

Now, you're going around with difficult feelings and a wound caused by the original experience, combined with other distressing feelings from trying to avoid your original feelings.

Unfortunately, you end up interacting with your external environment with unwanted feelings below the surface. And you risk them coming out toward another person at the wrong time.

Please don't push your feelings down and ignore them like they don't exist. You'll have to deal with them in another way that may be out of your control – like feeling angry to the point where self-awareness and understanding become difficult or impossible.

EXAMINING YOUR COGNITIVE DISTORTIONS

We all experience cognitive distortions daily. Cognitive distortions are negative thoughts, irrational beliefs, and habits that skew our perception of things. They play a crucial role in our cognitive processes. You aren't alone if you feel like you're in a loop of negative thinking.

Cognitive distortions make us exaggerate or view reality in a warped and unhealthy way. This can damage our relationships, mental health, and overall well-being. Let's discuss the different forms of cognitive distortions and how they affect you.

Aaron T. Beck was the first person to introduce us to the concept of cognitive distortions when he noticed dysfunctional thinking in his patients. But David Burns was the one who popularized the approach of identifying, correcting, and changing distorted thinking patterns to treat patients struggling with depression.

Negative thoughts and feelings exaggerate cognitive distortions. They convince you that your skewed thoughts are true, blinding you from reality. Unfortunately, these thought patterns are common and occur automatically in your everyday thoughts. This makes them hard to recognize and challenge, especially as they are wired into the brain.

One thing about the brain is that it likes shortcuts. Your brain remembers events from your past and will form a connection when you have similar thoughts or emotions in the present. Ordinarily, this is a good way to remember things (memory), but it's potentially dangerous for negative thoughts and feelings.

Habitual thinking can reinforce cognitive distortions, leading to increased anxiety, depression, and dysfunctional relationships. The following are four facts about cognitive distortions:

- All cognitive distortions are habitual ways of thinking or beliefs.
- They are false, exaggerated, and often inaccurate.
- They manifest as negative emotions or feelings.
- They can increase stress, anxiety, and depression, possibly causing psychological disorders.

There is no evidence that anxiety or depression causes cognitive distortions. Still, they are more common in people struggling with anxiety, depression, or other severe mental conditions.

The dysfunctional thought patterns are a product of the complex relationship between your thoughts, behaviors, and emotions. They don't have a specific root cause or an underlying reason. Instead, numerous factors, including social, cultural, and environmental factors, could contribute to these dysfunctional thinking patterns.

Social factors:

- Our social network and media can influence our beliefs, ideas, thoughts, and perceptions of ourselves and others.

- Dysfunctional social relationships can make us cultivate an "Us vs. Them" attitude.
- Parental guidance plays a key role in our mentality and attitude.
- Positive communication can promote healthy relationships and mental well-being.
- Active participation in social events may contribute to emotional and mental wellness.

Cultural factors:

- Customs, beliefs, religion, moral values, and language influence behavior.
- They influence how we communicate, behave, and handle our emotions.
- Culture impacts our willingness to express our emotions, speak up about our mental health, or seek help for a mental health issue.

Environmental factors:

- Accessibility to health care (physical and mental) services decreases stress and improves mental wellness.
- Genetics, financial status, and educational background influence our attitude, sense of security, persistence, and resilience.

These factors influence our upbringing, influencing our thoughts, emotions, and behaviors toward life events.

As noted, everyone experiences dysfunctional thinking patterns in their everyday thoughts. The mind operates on autopilot when we have cognitive distortions. Most people aren't negatively impacted; some can immediately recognize the unhelpful thoughts.

You don't realize that you are having these negative thoughts, making it incredibly hard to recognize that they are illogical and inaccurate. If you can't recognize faulty thinking, you reinforce them, which increases stress, anxiety, and depression, causing relationship problems and triggering other unwanted health issues.

We tend to assume that our feelings are caused by an event or something that happened to us. However, you don't jump from experiencing an event straight to emotion. Something plays a role in how you feel about the event or thing that happened to you – and that's your interpretation (thought) of the event. For example, "This thing happened and made me feel this way."

Below, we briefly discuss some of the most common cognitive distortions you might be experiencing.

- **"All or nothing" thinking**

This is also called polarized or "black and white" thinking. A person with this distortion believes that things are either this way or that way – no middle ground or a gray area. This cognitive distortion makes you think in extremes.

For example, a student used to being at the top of their class might feel like a failure if they fall to second place. The mentality is, *"If I'm not at the top of my class all the time, I am a total failure."*

- **Overgeneralization**

Overgeneralization is a pattern of thinking where you focus on a single event that you experienced and conclude based on that one piece of negative evidence. Then, since your conclusion is from that single event, you erroneously conclude that all similar events in the future will have the same negative outcome.

For example, a student falls to second place in their class for just one semester. Based on that, they conclude that they're a failure and will remain in second place for the rest of their life.

- **Mental Filtering**

This occurs when you focus solely on the negative aspect of a situation. This distortion is categorized into negative mental filtering and disqualifying the positive.

Negative mental filtering involves filtering out all the positives of a situation and fixating on the negatives. You magnify the negative details of the situation and dwell on the feelings they evoke. This can prevent you from seeing things as they are since you're focused on what went wrong rather than what worked.

For example, a subordinate receives an excellent review from their supervisor at work. Still, the person focuses on a single negative comment in the review.

Disqualifying the positive, on the other hand, acknowledges the positive aspect of the situation but rejects it. It is an absolute rejection of one's positive experiences. This cognitive distortion makes you invalidate and dismiss the positives as you try to find ways to make them negative.

For example, the subordinate who got an excellent review at work overlooks their manager's pause and tries to explain it away as a fluke rather than a product of their hard work.

- **Mind reading**

This occurs when you think you know what another person is thinking. It is based purely on your assumptions with zero physical evidence. You assume you know people's intentions and reasons for doing what they do and conclude that is the only valid reason. You also fail to acknowledge the other possibilities.

For example, you're on a lunch date with your friend, but they seem disinterested. You automatically conclude they don't want to spend time with you. In reality, it could be that they feel discomforted or have hundreds of other reasons that have nothing to do with you.

- **Fortune telling**

This distortion is similar to mind reading because it's also based purely on assumptions. You jump to conclusions or make predictions with little to no evidence. The conclusion or prediction almost always has a negative outcome.

For example, you're about to go on a date with someone you like, but you're pretty sure the date will go horribly. You make predictions that aren't based on actual evidence.

- **Catastrophizing**

You catastrophize when you exaggerate or minimize the magnitude of an event. Exaggerating (magnification) escalates negative thoughts and makes you assume the worst-case scenario. It occurs when there are unknowns about a situation you can't control.

For example, you're meeting someone for a date. However, that person is running late, so you start assuming the worst – "Maybe they don't like me after all" or "They are probably out with someone else." But there are other reasonable explanations for your date's lateness.

On the other hand, minimizing the magnitude of an event occurs when you diminish your positive experiences.

For example, you are promoted at work but fail to acknowledge the accomplishment. You diminish the importance of the promotion because *"It's not a big deal; other people were promoted."*

- **Labeling**

This is a more extreme form of overgeneralization. Instead of recognizing it as a mistake or a one-time thing, you label the person involved. This kind of thinking makes you judge yourself and others based on a single negative experience.

For example, you label your coworker a "selfish jerk" because they couldn't help you with a task, even though they might have been occupied with their work.

- **Personalization**

Ever met someone who takes everything personally? If yes, that's due to a cognitive distortion called personalization – the tendency to take things personally. This negative thinking pattern makes you feel directly or personally attacked by other people's words and actions, even when unrelated to you.

For example, you attend a work luncheon where everyone interacts with others except you. As such, you feel like everybody at your workplace hates you. This makes you think your coworkers are discriminating against you.

- **Blaming**

This faulty thinking occurs when you blame others for your problems. It's similar to personalization, but the difference is that you award blame to external factors. Rather than taking responsibility, you assume the victim role and blame others for your pain.

For example, you blame your partner for a conflict instead of sharing the responsibility for things you both did. You assume you're the victim and your partner intentionally hurts you.

- **Emotional reasoning**

Whatever emotion you feel in response to a situation must be true. Unfortunately, this distortion makes you treat your feelings as facts by blocking your ability to reason logically. As a result, you incorrectly assume that the negative feeling evoked by your emotion is the only truth that matters.

For example, you feel lonely because your friends are at a resort for the weekend, and you can't go. But from this feeling, you conclude that people don't want to be around you. Your thought: *"My friends would have stayed here if they cared about me."*

There are other cognitive distortions, but the ones I've just discussed are commonly addressed with CBT.

Becoming aware of cognitive distortions and their impact on your thinking is the key to overcoming negative thinking.

Now that you're well familiar with how the brain is wired, you are one step closer to learning how to rewire your brain and overcome negative thoughts. But, more importantly, it will be easier to learn how to change your emotions by addressing your cognition and behavior.

Chapter Two Highlights

- Thoughts, emotions, and behaviors are linked, and they all affect each other. You can change how you feel by addressing how you think and act. Learn to identify the thoughts that trigger your behaviors, and you'll be able to handle your feelings better.
- Cognitive distortions (faulty thinking patterns) are often false, exaggerated, and inaccurate. However, paying attention to them can result in chronic stress, anxiety, and depression and possibly cause other psychological issues. Therefore, figuring out faulty thinking patterns to eliminate them is a part of the CBT program.
- Cognitive errors disrupt your perception of life experiences, giving you an irrationally negative outlook on life. This can damage your mental health and well-being. However, you can overcome negative thinking by eliminating distortions in your cognitive processes.
- Culture influences how you handle emotions, act, and interact with people. Cultural factors, such as language, customs, religion, etc., affect how you express yourself and your willingness to speak to others about your mental health issues. Examine any factor that may be hindering the treatment process for you.
- Don't ignore or push your feelings down, as that can make them spiral out of control, thus increasing your distress. Instead, emotional self-awareness should be a regular part of your daily life.

HOW TO EFFECTIVELY REWIRE THE BRAIN

B ack when I struggled with negative thoughts, it felt like I was constantly dipping my feet into quicksand and sinking deeper and deeper until I was completely buried under. That is how I felt, especially with how the thoughts weighed on my mind daily. All it took was a single negative thought for my mind to spiral out of control. Before I could even say Jack Robinson, I found myself in a negative loop.

I felt hopeless and didn't see a way out of my situation. I was like a spider caught in my own web, except this was a web of strong, self-defeating beliefs and intense distress. Naturally, most people in my social circle withdrew from me. Nobody wanted to be around me, thanks to the demons in my head as I constantly lashed out.

At one point, I was convinced that I was fighting real demons. In a way, you could say that I was, but I didn't know that they were pesky little thoughts in the subconscious of my mind. Of course, I tried to deal with the thoughts by pushing them to the back of my mind. The more I tried this, the harder it was for me to fight them off – and they eventually took hold of my mind.

That was until CBT taught me to recognize my dysfunctional thinking patterns. And subsequently, using CBT techniques, I rewired my brain to overcome automatic negative thoughts and reframe my thought processes into producing healthier thinking patterns.

WHAT ARE AUTOMATIC NEGATIVE THOUGHTS (ANTS)?

How many negative thoughts pop into your head daily? How many have sneaked into your mind since you started this journey? Would you have a specific number if you paid attention and counted? Perhaps you've thought, *"This book won't help me. Nothing will help me. I am destined to be depressed all my life."*

Automatic negative thoughts come out of nowhere. For example, you're minding your business one minute, and out of nowhere, you're thinking:

"I'm a failure."

"I could have been more productive this week."

"I won't achieve my goals."

"I'm destined to be unsuccessful."

You probably wouldn't allow a friend or a random person to sneak up behind you and say these things to you. But every day, you let these dysfunctional thoughts rule your head and dictate your mood, decisions, and life. Unfortunately, the longer you give them power over your thought process, the harder it is to seize back control and rewire your brain to approach life with a positive outlook.

Automatic negative thoughts are self-explanatory. They are unwanted and negative thoughts that disturb your mind without a conscious effort. This is why you don't even realize they are there unless you deliberately look for them. One thing about ANTs is they don't even have to be related to your current situation to appear in your head.

ANTs are involuntary responses based on your core beliefs about yourself, others, and the world. They can influence your mood in such a powerful way and create self-doubt, irritability, anger, anxiety, and depression.

Individuals struggling with anxiety and depression experience automatic negative thoughts, but these thoughts vary from person to person, depending on their cognitive distortions.

Generally, though, all automatic negative thoughts are:

- Negative
- Self-sabotaging
- Invasive and uninvited
- Biased because they distort your view of reality
- Easy to believe

Coincidentally, the "ANTs" acronym is undeniably appropriate because, like ants, automatic negative thoughts are intrusive, unwanted, and capable of ruining your picnic or, in this case, your life. Buddha once said, *"Nothing can harm you as much as your thoughts."* And for people dealing with ANTs, this is undoubtedly true.

First, I should make it clear that it is perfectly normal to have negative thoughts. One of the mistakes I made when I started practicing CBT techniques was trying to erase all of my negative thoughts all at once. I eventually learned just how unrealistic that was.

The earlier humans survived the jungle by constantly looking out for threats, attending to problems as they arose, and learning from their mistakes. Imagination is one of the best qualities of your mind, and it exists for you to imagine potential problems and threats. That allows you to solve problems before they spiral out of your control.

But this quality of imagination also works against you by making your mind a *"random negative thought generator."* Your mind will use cognitive distortions to convince you of things that aren't true and make you believe them. So, guess what... It's all in your mind.

Automatic negative thoughts overwhelm your mind when negative thinking becomes habitual. Stats show that 90% of our daily thoughts are repetitive. That means you recycle the same thoughts over and over each day; you'll have almost similar thoughts today as you had yesterday and the day before.

When you have a negative or positive experience, your brain remembers it. If you have a similar experience another time, your brain triggers a negative response believing there's a threat. That response is what evokes anxiety, anger, depression, or agitation. And it can create a downward spiral toward a never-ending cycle of negative thoughts, emotions, and dysfunctional behavior.

If you indulge in negative thinking often enough, your brain creates a neural pathway. The more you engage in it, the stronger that connection becomes. That is how we form habits and why breaking a bad habit can be difficult.

But since I said automatic negative thoughts are normal and exist to ensure our survival, why are they so toxic and harmful?

Negative thinking patterns induce stress, which changes the brain in many ways. Every negative thought your mind produces alters the chemical composition of your brain, causing a cascade of negative effects that extend to emotion and behavior.

Some of the negative effects of ANTs include:

- Depleting feel-good brain chemicals such as dopamine and serotonin
- Slowing the release of brain-derived neurotrophic factor (BDNF), a protein involved in forming new brain cells
- Enlarging the size of your amygdala (the brain's fear center) while shrinking the size of your brain
- Accelerating the aging process
- Increasing your risk of psychiatric and neurodegenerative conditions

Automatic negative thoughts put the brain under chronic stress, changing it to its DNA level. You might not know this yet, but chronic stress is directly linked to anxiety, depression, and other mental health conditions.

Suppose you're struggling with anxiety. In that case, you might have negative thoughts about the future. You might tell yourself:

- *"I will make a fool of myself at the interview."*
- *"The company is going to reject me."*
- *"My whole class will laugh at me when I fumble my presentation."*

These thoughts, usually set in the future, are about things that haven't even happened yet. Although you don't know what the outcome of your situation will be, ANTs convince you that things won't go well with zero or illogical evidence. Your thoughts aren't supported by reality or logic, yet they compel you to live in fear and avoid certain situations.

For example, if you have social anxiety, you might have automatic negative thoughts that convince you to avoid social situations.

Not all ANTs are based on predicting the future. Many negative thoughts focus on the self and the past. Some of these ANTs may pop up like:

- *"I'm unworthy and unlovable."*
- *"I don't deserve to be happy."*

- *"Everyone hates me."*
- *"I make everything so much worse."*

These thoughts can overwhelm you with feelings of helplessness and hopelessness and can be exhausting.

Automatic negative thoughts aren't productive. They don't do anything except make you feel bad about yourself. So why does your brain keep allowing them to pop into your head? Like ANTs themselves, the answer to this question varies.

You're a meaning-making creature. You want answers and make decisions pretty quickly. Sometimes, the easiest way to get an answer is to blame yourself or others. You might find it easier to attribute guilt to yourself rather than put the blame on a larger history.

The mind also wants a quick fix or answer. You may find it easier to "predict the future" than to wait for it to arrive. It's much easier to dismiss yourself as a failure rather than accept that you, like everyone else, are bound to make mistakes. Unfortunately, you can't magically make ANTs disappear. Remember, when a negative thought pattern is repeated long enough, it metamorphoses into rumination.

THE RELATIONSHIP BETWEEN ANTS AND RUMINATION

We all enjoy music. You can probably relate to the hook of a catchy song getting stuck in your head. Even though you may not like the song or artist, you find yourself thinking about it for longer than you'd like – an earworm, as we say. This can be a pleasant experience for the most part.

However, when it's a thought, specifically a negative one, the experience is far less pleasant. When automatic negative thoughts begin to spiral, you can get stuck in a loop of repetitive negative thinking, otherwise called rumination.

Rumination is the habit of continuously engaging in repetitive negative thought processes without end. The cycle can be distressing, difficult to break, and often involves thinking over and over about a negative thought or evasive problem.

Rumination consumes much mental and emotional energy, which can negatively impact your mental well-being. It can present itself as worrying about the future, obsessing over the past, or trying to forecast how a situation might play out. But, sometimes, it's just you experiencing the same thought in a loop without variation.

Rumination is a co-occurring symptom in many mental health problems like anxiety and depression. It is a defining symptom of Obsessive Compulsive Disorder (OCD). You could say that rumination is a compulsion because you can't help yourself, despite being unaware of the thoughts.

For a depressed person, the rumination theme usually borders on being inadequate. However, when rumination is based on anxiety, you get stuck because the recurring negative thoughts encourage you to pursue questions you can't answer and truths you don't know.

Rumination is usually addressed from an OCD perspective. By definition, compulsion is something you do to reduce the distress caused by unwanted, intrusive thoughts. But rumination is often misinterpreted and rarely addressed as a compulsion.

This is because we erroneously assume that compulsions can only be observable actions or behaviors, like washing hands or checking the gas repeatedly to ensure it's switched off. However, rumination is a mental compulsion that happens internally, which is why other people can't observe it.

For example, someone with contamination OCD gets the compulsion to wash their hands repeatedly – that is an observable action. Conversely, someone with OCD relating to existential themes gets the compulsion to ruminate on things such as life, meaning, etc. In both cases, the compulsions (ritual hand washing and rumination) are responses to an unwanted, intrusive thought.

Although rumination exists to solve a problem, it can become problematic in its own right. Rumination can sometimes feel out of control. Those who ruminate may only realize what they are doing once a significant amount of time has passed, and they have spiraled far down the rabbit hole.

In fact, you may not be aware that you are stuck in that spiral of negative thinking. Still, it's an act you compulsively engage in rather than just an automatic negative thought that conveniently pops up.

The key to stopping rumination is recognizing the difference between actively thinking about something and simply "having a thought" about that thing. A negative thought becomes "rumination" when you turn that thought over in your mind and over-engage with it to a fault instead of leaving it in your subconscious.

STOP FALLING FOR NEGATIVITY BIAS

Negativity bias is a cognitive bias that makes the brain focus more on negatives than positives. The human tendency is to register negative events more readily than positive ones while dwelling on them. You feel it more intensely when someone criticizes rather than praises you.

As humans, we are wired to:

- Remember negative experiences more accurately than positive ones.
- Recall criticism better than praise, even if it is constructive.
- React more intensely to negative stimuli.
- Ruminate about negative events more frequently than positive ones.
- React more strongly to negative experiences than to equally positive ones.

Negativity bias is why bad impressions are much more difficult to overcome than good ones. It is also why traumatic experiences from our past have such lasting effects throughout our lives. In your interactions, you're more likely to notice the negative bits and recall them more vividly in the future.

For example, I remember having a great day at work due to the reception of my contribution to a group project. It was great until a coworker who was also part of the project gave me a backhanded compliment that I found pretty insulting. I was already struggling with recurring negative thoughts, so I spent the rest of that workday and the week fixating on the offhand comment.

When I met a friend later that day for dinner, she asked how my day was, and my reply was "pretty awful" – even though it was a good day by all ramifications.

When I began my CBT journey, I learned about negativity bias and how it can lead us to pay more attention to the seemingly bad events in our lives, magnifying their importance and making them much bigger than they should be.

Psychological research has established that human beings tend to focus more on the negative as we explore and try to make sense of the world. This is because we are wired to believe a negative piece of news over a positive one.

Your human nature makes the risk of losing seem greater than the chance of winning – even though, in reality, the potential benefit outweighs the cost. For instance, if I gave you a chance to win $150 or lose $100 with equal probability, you would most likely choose to pass on the opportunity. But why?

This has to do with the link between negativity bias and loss aversion. This cognitive bias outlines how the pain of losing something is twice as powerful as the joy of winning or gaining something.

Negativity bias makes us:

- Pay more attention to negative events
- Seek lessons in negative experiences and outcomes
- Make a decision based on negative data rather than positive information

"Bad things" grab our attention more and stick to our memories for a long time. And in many cases, they influence our perceptions of the world and our decisions.

Psychological research shows that negativity bias drives motivation to complete tasks. You are less motivated to complete a task when the incentive is framed as something you gain than when it's framed to help you avoid losing something. For example, your job.

This affects how motivated we are to pursue our goals. Rather than think about what you'll gain if you work toward something, you're likely to focus on what you might have to give up to achieve that same goal. Plus, research shows that we're more likely to accept negative news as truthful.

This human tendency to focus more on bad things and dismiss or overlook good things is understandable from an evolutionary point of view. In earlier times, paying attention to threats and dangerous things was the thin line between life and death.

Our ancestors, who were more attuned to danger, had higher chances of survival than others. This is because constant awareness of threats and danger was necessary to stay alive. But even though we no longer face the same threats or dangers as our early ancestors, our brain still pays extra attention to "danger" to keep us safe.

Today, we no longer need to be on constant alert to survive, but that bias toward the negative still plays a vital role in the functioning of our brains. Research has shown that bias can have a range of effects on how we think, feel, and respond to stimuli.

Your relationships are some of the areas of your life where you might feel the impact of negativity bias. It can prompt you to always expect the worst from people, especially in intimate relationships where you've known the other person for a long time.

For example, I used to anticipate negative reactions whenever I had something to discuss with my partner. This made me approach our conversations defensively, leading to arguments and resentment.

Regarding your interpersonal relationships (family, friends, lovers, coworkers, etc.), it helps to remember that negative comments hold more weight than positive ones. It also helps if you're aware of your tendency to preoccupy yourself with the negative.

Negativity bias also affects your decision-making process. Kahneman and Tversky, two Nobel-winning researchers, found that humans tend to place greater weight on the negative aspect of an experience than the positive, especially when making a decision. Also, when forming an impression of other people, you're likely to fixate on negative data.

The good thing is negative biases are no different than ANTs and rumination. You can overcome all three by reframing how you think. So, how do you do that?

HOW TO REFRAME NEGATIVE THOUGHTS IN NINE STEPS

You can reframe negative thinking patterns in nine steps. Over time, you'll find that your mind has switched to a more rational way of thinking.

- Stop the cycle
- Breathe
- Recognize that you are not your thoughts
- Distract the mind
- Interrupt the cycle with self-care
- Challenge the thought
- Know your triggers
- Journal
- Practice gratitude

Now, let's take a deeper look at each step.

1. Stop the cycle

If you find yourself stuck in a loop of negative thoughts, pay attention to when the thoughts sneak into your mind and stop them. Awareness is a vital first step for stopping a negative thought on its track and then challenging it. So, pause for a moment and observe what you're thinking – you'll find it isn't right. Then, isolate that thought and focus on it. This is called metacognition. You realize, "Hey, this thinking isn't quite accurate." Remember to breathe and relax in your body. ANT can make you disassociate from your body.

2. Breathe

Once you're aware of your dysfunctional thought and isolated it, separate it from who you are. Empowering yourself to challenge negative thoughts by taking small, brave actions would be best. In this second step, that action is to slow down your breath by inhaling more deeply. The goal is to interrupt your sympathetic nervous system, which is in charge of your body's "fight or flight" response.

Deep breathing activates the parasympathetic nervous system, inducing a sense of calm and relaxation. So, inhale deeply and exhale slowly to release the tension in your body. Pay attention to the sound of your breath. Visualize it flowing into your body and lighting up your cells.

3. Recognize that you aren't your thoughts

Remember that thoughts are not facts. You are a separate entity from your thoughts. Rather than succumb to the negative thinking pattern, use the sense of discomfort to remind yourself of your true strengths.

When you practice deep breathing, you'll become painfully aware of the internal chatter, the noise, labeling, and narrating by that voice in your head. I learned to be a passive observer of my thoughts, and you can do the same. It helped me become more aware that I am not my thoughts.

But you'll also realize that you aren't your thoughts. So the next time you feel overwhelmed by negative thoughts, remember that you're capable of streamlining the process because you're in charge. The moment you do that can be very powerful.

4. Distract the mind

The intensity of automatic negative thoughts can be quite frightening. The frustrating thing is these thoughts are on autopilot, so you aren't consciously aware of them. By focusing on problem-solving, you can distract your mind from the buzz and chatter of negative thoughts.

Don't believe your thoughts. You may be depressed, but you are also a problem solver. Remember that you can break the cycle by finding a healthy distraction to keep your mind occupied.

5. Interrupt the cycle with self-care

Automatic negative thoughts put the body in a constant state of stress and hypervigilance. And depression can make all sorts of unreasonable demands from the body. When you fixate on a negative experience, seize that opportunity to do something engaging and enjoyable.

Respond to that by breathing. Find something that can make you feel good; do something nice for yourself. Practice self-care and self-compassion regularly.

6. Challenge your thoughts

"Where is the evidence?"

This is an important question you must pose to your mind when an automatic negative thought pops up. There is power in questioning your thoughts. ANTs trigger powerful emotions, but that doesn't make them true or logical. Interrupt your thought to assess if it's factual to stop the cycle of rumination.

Suppose a thought such as, "I am going to fail," arises in your head. Instead of letting that thought go on unchallenged, interrupt it with a "huh?" Then, look within to see if any evidence supports the negative statement.

If you look into that thought, you'll probably find no substance.

7. Know your triggers

Work on identifying your triggers so you can know when a negative thought is about to arise. It prepares you to challenge and question the thought. Perhaps you're alone or with someone. What time is it? Did something happen in particular that you can point to? Or is there an event preceding an influx of negative thoughts in your daily life?

That leads to the next point.

8. Journal

Journaling is an excellent way to track your negative thoughts' triggers. Keeping a journal is straightforward. Make it simple and go straight to the point. Be as detailed as possible when you write down the things that trigger you.

9. Practice Gratitude

Create a list of things you're genuinely grateful for, particularly activities you enjoy. You don't have to make it complicated – even the simplest things matter. Your gratitude journal can uplift your mood when you feel low and depressed. Be sure to include a ton of uplifting activities and memories.

Exercise for Challenging Negative Thoughts

Below is a list of questions to challenge intrusive and unhelpful thoughts. Use this list alongside your *"Thought journal."*

- *Are there facts to support this thought? Is there contradictory evidence to refute it?*
- *If this thought were true, what would be the worst possible outcome?*
- *Am I generalizing based on a past event?*
- *Can I view this from a positive perspective?*
- *How can I deal with this scenario effectively?*
- *Am I ready to accept aspects of this event or situation?*
- *Is this still within my control?*
- *Are my thoughts aggravating the situation?*
- *Besides myself, who or what else might affect my reaction to this situation?*

You can also come up with some questions on your own.

As mentioned earlier, stress is the primary source of many people's anxiety, depression, and other mental health problems. Unfortunately, you might have grown up believing that stress is something you should just put up with as a part of everyday life. But the consequences of accepting that can wreak havoc on your physical and mental health.

Before you begin to address your problems with CBT techniques, you must learn healthy ways to cope with stress. And that's precisely what I'll be discussing in the next chapter.

Stay with me!

Chapter Three Highlights

- Negative thoughts are automatic and intrusive. They are based on the beliefs you have about yourself, the people around you, and the world at large. Allowing negative thoughts to run in your head unopposed can destabilize your feelings and behavior. Therefore, it's important to constantly challenge negative thought patterns.
- Anxiety and depression are characterized by rumination – a habit of repeating negative thought patterns endlessly. This can cause distress and consume your emotional and mental energy. However, you can stop rumination by making a conscious decision not to engage with negative thoughts.
- Negativity bias wires you to commit negative experiences to memory far more often than positive ones. Breaking this bias can change your attitude toward your positive or negative experiences. It also teaches you to react to them in healthier ways.
- A vital part of the CBT program is learning to reframe negative thoughts into more rational and positive ones. Your thoughts are just thoughts – they are neither factual nor accurate. It's OK to challenge and question them instead of just accepting them.
- Journaling can help you track negative thoughts and monitor how they trigger unpleasant feelings. In addition, it can make it easier to challenge or support these thoughts based on available evidence. Essentially, this is how you rewire the brain.

4

GETTING A GRIP ON STRESS

Stress may not technically be a disease, but it can impact your physical and mental health in ways you could never imagine. And it may shock you to know just how prevalent stress is in America and around the world. Unfortunately, despite how hard we try, stress remains part of life, something we can only learn to tolerate.

Stress is a response – your body's way of physically, emotionally, and mentally reacting to stressors. Often, stress is triggered in response to change – a new job, a big move, a divorce, a wedding, etc. But the source of stress may also be a person's environment, such as a toxic workplace or a relationship conflict.

When a perceived threat confronts the brain, the body releases cortisol (the stress hormone), epinephrine, and norepinephrine, increasing stress levels. This also increases blood pressure, tense muscles, and alertness. You may know this as the "fight or flight" response. However, in many cases, the source of stress isn't a physical aggressor, which can cause headaches, lack of sleep, increased muscle tension, and several other symptoms.

I had no idea how common stress was until I discovered many stats that blew my mind. There's barely anyone who can completely escape stress. We all deal with stress in our way.

Short bursts of this response can help us boost productivity or improve focus. For example, stress enables you to get that due assignment done right before the deadline. It makes you think, "I work better under pressure."

In contrast, chronic stress contributes to health problems such as high blood pressure, anxiety disorders, depression, heart disease, and gastrointestinal disorders.

So, how common is stress in the United States?

- 49% of U.S. adults report that stress negatively impacts their behavior.
- 80% of American employees report feeling stressed on the job.
- Over 75% of Americans reported headaches, fatigue, sleep disturbances, and other stress symptoms.
- 63% of American adults are stressed about the economy. Yet, ironically, workplace stress robs the economy of over $300 billion annually – which doesn't help the economy.

It's tempting to believe that stress is only an annoyance that visits and leaves with some events. But the reality is that short-term and long-term stress can have an immediate and prolonged impact on a person's overall well-being. So stress should not be dismissed, and you're about to learn why.

WHY STRESS SHOULD NOT BE DISMISSED

The effect of stress on your health and well-being cannot be overstated. A 2013 study published in The Journal of the American Medical Association (JAMA) suggests that 60-80% of primary care hospital visits are linked to stress. Every condition and symptom can be worsened by stress in the body. And if you want to know what part of the body stress is experienced, the answer is straightforward: every part. You'll agree that this doesn't seem like something anyone should want to dismiss.

Your nervous system is connected to every tissue in your body. Thus, when the stress side of your nervous system becomes overactive, it affects every part of your body. If there is already a disorder going on in a specific organ system, it could be aggravated by the stress response,

Unfortunately, that makes the list of diseases and conditions that can be worsened by stress as long as the complete list of diagnoses – thousands of medical conditions. Common conditions can be present at all times, whereas other conditions happen, depending on the time of year.

For example, gastrointestinal disorders can be diagnosed all year round. Meanwhile, respiratory illnesses become prevalent in the winter because stress impairs the immune system.

Stress naturally occurs when we cannot cope with specific events or demands. Often, these demands come from relationships, work, financial troubles, and other situations. But it's caused by anything that poses a real or perceived threat to your well-being. Ultimately, stress is a natural response that is integral to survival.

The fight-or-flight response is your body's way of telling you that something needs attention or action as soon as possible. It tells you when and how to respond to danger. So, being in tune with that part of you is crucial.

But it becomes too easy to trigger when the body remains in fight-or-flight mode for a long time. This also happens when there are too many external stressors at a time. The result is that your mental and physical health becomes vulnerable to attacks.

You should be familiar with the two types of stress below:

- **Acute stress:** is the type of stress we all experience. It is short-term, and it goes away as quickly as it comes. That is the stress you feel when you find yourself in traffic on your way to work or when you have an argument with your spouse. Acute stress exists to help us cope with dangerous situations. We also experience it when we do something exciting. But, again, everyone experiences acute stress at one time or another.
- **Chronic stress:** is long-term stress that negatively affects the body. Any stress that remains for weeks or months is considered chronic stress. For example, you

may struggle with chronic stress if you have financial troubles, an unhappy relationship, or work troubles. It's easy to become used to chronic stress to the point where you don't even know it's a problem. And that's how it always eventually leads to health complications.

One thing about stress is that it manifests differently in everyone. We all react differently to stressors. Personally, simply thinking about a stressor can trigger stress. However, something that is a source of stress for you may not affect another person in that same way, and nearly any event can act as a stressor.

Science does not yet have a reason why the same stressor may induce different degrees of stress in two people. However, it's been established that anxiety, depression, and other mental health conditions can make some people more susceptible to stress responses than others.

Past experiences may influence how you react to triggers. Common events that can serve as stressors include:

- Employment issues
- Lack of money or time
- Illness
- Moving to a new home
- Unhappy relationship or marriage
- Divorce
- Grief or bereavement
- Family problems

Other commonly reported stressors are:

- Pregnancy or becoming a first-time parent
- Pregnancy loss
- Fear of accidents
- Fear of crime
- Problematic neighbors
- Excessive noise and overcrowding
- Uncertainty about the future or outcome of an important event

One may experience ongoing stress in response to a traumatic event, such as abuse or an accident.

When the body triggers a stress response, it slows down bodily functions, including the ones performed by the digestive and immune systems. This happens so that the body can focus on alertness, breathing, and blood flow and also prepare (tense) the muscles for emergency use.

Some of the changes that occur in your body during a stress response include:

- Pulse and blood pressure rise
- Increased breathing
- Decrease in immune activity
- Delayed digestive function
- Decrease in sleepiness due to hyperalertness

Your reaction to a difficult or uncomfortable situation determines the impact of stress on your overall health. Some people don't have a severe stress response even when exposed to multiple stressors simultaneously, whereas others react strongly to a single stressor.

A person who feels like they don't have the resources to cope effectively with stress will most likely react strongly to stressors, potentially causing health problems. Stressors affect everyone differently.

Some generally acknowledged positive experiences can cause stress, such as traveling, getting a promotion, getting married, having a baby, or moving to a bigger, better home.

This is because these positive events are rooted in significant change. They involve new responsibilities, extra effort, and adapting to new environments. They also require you to step into new territories. As you probably know, the unknown can be terrifying.

While you're looking forward to your promotion at work, you may be excessively worried about your ability to handle the new responsibilities that come with the promotion. So, a situation does not have to be negative to harm your health and mood.

It's not helpful to dismiss stress because it can adversely affect your overall health and well-being. Stress can make life's usual hassles more challenging to manage. You realize the importance of your mind-body connection when you examine how stress impacts your life.

When the brain (mind) experiences significant stress levels, the body responds accordingly. Feeling stressed over money, interpersonal relationships, or your living condition can create literal health problems. The inverse of this is also true. Dealing with health problems like diabetes or high blood pressure can skyrocket your stress levels.

Here are examples of stress-influenced conditions:

- Diabetes
- Heart disease
- Obesity
- Ulcers
- Sexual dysfunction
- Hyperthyroidism
- Alopecia (hair loss)
- Tooth and gum disease

CHECK YOUR STRESS SYMPTOMS

The body's reaction to a stressor is to release hormones. And as I noted earlier, these hormones make your muscles tense, increase your breathing, and make you more alert, which causes different physical, emotional, and behavioral symptoms within. The scary part is that you may not even realize that these symptoms are affecting your health.

Perhaps you think that your nagging headache or lack of focus, or decreased productivity at work is being caused by your illness. In reality, stress may be the actual true cause. But you will only know that if you're familiar with the different symptoms of stress.

Stress symptoms affect your thoughts, feelings, and behaviors, and if left unchecked, it can result in many of the health problems I outlined previously. Learning to recognize common symptoms is the first step toward managing them.

Physical symptoms of stress include:

- Headaches
- Sweating
- Back or chest pain
- Muscle cramps or spasms
- Stomach upset
- Weight loss or gain
- Constipation or diarrhea
- Aches and pains in different parts of the body
- A decline in sex drive
- Sleep problems

Emotional symptoms of stress include:

- Anxiety
- Lack of focus
- Irritability
- Anger
- Restlessness
- Sadness or depression
- Feeling overwhelmed
- Forgetfulness
- Burnout
- Fatigue

- Feeling insecure

Behavioral symptoms of stress include:

- Food cravings (undereating or overeating)
- Angry outbursts
- Social withdrawal
- Tobacco misuse
- Alcohol and drug misuse
- Frequent crying or whining
- Reduced exercise
- More relationship conflicts

You can watch out for these signs to know when you're dealing with prolonged stress. If you notice these symptoms, taking steps for effective stress management is essential. There are various stress management strategies that you can use, and I'll be discussing a few of them.

DIAPHRAGMATIC BREATHING

The diaphragm is a muscle at the base of your lungs, regarded as the most efficient organ for breathing. There is breathing, and then there is diaphragmatic breathing. As you can probably tell, the two are worlds apart.

Diaphragmatic breathing involves utilizing the diaphragm more accurately when you breathe. These benefits reduce blood pressure and heart rate and promote relaxation. In addition, it manages the physical symptoms of stress, which also improves your emotional and behavioral symptoms.

This breathing technique:

- Strengthens the diaphragm
- Slows your breathing to make it more impactful on the body
- Decreases oxygen demand
- Utilizes less energy and effort to breathe

Our normal breathing doesn't utilize our lungs to their full capacity. But you can achieve this with diaphragmatic breathing and ultimately increase lung efficiency. Diaphragmatic breathing requires you to take deep breaths with your diaphragm consciously.

You may or may not already be familiar with diaphragmatic breathing through other names such as abdominal breathing, belly breathing, etc.

This breathing technique offers many benefits, including:

- Inducing relaxation
- Improving muscle function during a workout
- Increasing oxygen presence in the blood
- Improving the ease of passing gas waste from the lungs
- Reducing heart rate
- Reducing blood pressure

Diaphragmatic breathing can help you manage any condition that affects your breathing, such as stress, anxiety, asthma, COPD, etc. You can combine the technique with any treatments recommended by your doctor or healthcare provider.

There are two ways to do the diaphragmatic breathing technique: lying down and sitting. Let's look at these individually.

Here are four steps to try diaphragmatic breathing (lying down):

1. Lie flat on your back in bed or on a flat surface, with your knees bent and your head supported with a pillow. You can place a pillow beneath your knees to support your legs.
2. Put one hand on your chest and the other under your rib cage. That will allow you to feel the movement of your diaphragm as you breathe in and out.
3. Take a deep breath slowly through your nose. You should feel your stomach move out and the hand on your chest rise. Ensure your hand remains still on your upper chest.
4. Tighten the muscles in your stomach to push your belly back in, ensuring your hand lowers as you breathe out through pursed lips. Your hand should remain firmly on your chest.

You might want to practice the "lying down" technique a few times before you try it while sitting down.

To perform diaphragmatic breathing while sitting, follow these instructions.

1. Sit in a chair that makes you feel as comfortable as possible, with your knees bent. Relax your shoulders, neck, and head.
2. Place one hand on your chest and just under your rib cage to feel the diaphragm's movement as you inhale and exhale.
3. Take a deep breath slowly through your nose. Ensure the hand on your chest stays firmly in the same place. You should feel your stomach move out and your hands rise.
4. Tighten the muscles in your stomach to push your belly back in as you breathe out through pursed lips. Your hand should remain as still as possible on your chest.

Diaphragmatic breathing becomes easier the more you practice. At first, it will take a lot of effort, and you'll get tired easily. But it will become automatic if you keep at it. You can start with 5-10 minutes of practice about three or four times daily. Gradually increase your practice time and make it harder by placing a book on your stomach if you're up to it.

Stress breathing is another technique you can use to relieve stress or anxiety. It can help induce instant relaxation in any distressing or uncomfortable situation. It's also a great way to heat your body. With this strategy, you can pull in and store energy in your body on demand.

Here is the stress breath exercise in four steps:

1. Breathe in slowly and deeply and make it audible. You should feel the sound vibrating at the back of your throat.
2. Hold your breath and slowly bring your chin toward your chest. Now, count back from five.
3. Breathe out (audibly through the nose) as you slowly raise your head back up.
4. That's one complete cycle. Now, repeat steps 1 to 2 twelve times in a row.

Practice the stress breath daily during the day and at nighttime.

PROGRESSIVE MUSCLE RELAXATION (PMR)

The benefits of PMR are endless. PMR helps release tension buildup in the muscles and body. In turn, helping you manage stress and anxiety, all while relieving you from insomnia and reducing chronic pain symptoms.

This relaxation technique involves the simple exercise of tightening your muscle groups one at a time and then relaxing them to release the knots and tension in those muscles. Healthcare providers typically combine progressive muscle relaxation with standard treatments to relieve symptoms for conditions such as headaches, high blood pressure, digestive problems, and cancer pain.

I learned to use PMR to relieve acute stress instantly, so it doesn't build up and become chronic stress - you can too. My favorite thing about this technique is that you only need 10 to 20 minutes of daily practice to check your stress levels.

The best way to practice PMR is to tense and relax one muscle group at a time in a linear order, beginning with the lower part of your body and moving up to the abdomen, chest, and face. Like diaphragmatic breathing, you can do this seated or lying down. Ensure you wear comfortable clothing and practice quietly with no distractions.

Here's how to perform progressive muscle relaxation:

1. Take a few deep breaths to relax your body and prepare your muscles.
2. While breathing in, tighten the first muscle group (perhaps your feet) as much as possible. Wait for ten seconds, then exhale and suddenly relax that muscle group.
3. Stay in relaxation mode for 10-20 seconds before moving on to the next muscle group (for example, your legs).
4. When you release the tension in your muscles, focus on the changes within the affected muscle group. You could visualize the tension flowing out of your body as you do each group.
5. Work your way up until you've contracted and relaxed all muscle groups in your body.

As a beginner in progressive muscle relaxation, I found the following tips helpful.

- Set aside 15-20 minutes to practice every day. Choose a quiet, comfortable part of your home.
- Switch off all your gadgets to avoid being distracted during the exercise.
- Do not hold your breath, as that will only cause unneeded tension.
- Inhale deeply when you tighten your muscles and exhale deeply when you release them.
- Follow any sequence that works best for you. For example, you can start at the head and move down the body if you find that more effective.
- Practice this exercise even when you're calm and relaxed. That will make it easier to master stressful or difficult times.
- Finally, wear loose clothing to ensure you're as comfortable as possible.

In the beginning, listening to PMR recordings during the exercise is helpful. That way, you can follow instructions without thinking about them constantly. But, of course, that also helps you avoid distractions.

Research has shown that PMR has many benefits, including stress and anxiety relief. The best thing is you can practice in the comfort of your home or even in your car. So be sure to practice regularly. Over time, you'll feel more relaxed and calmer physically and mentally.

GUIDED MEDITATION FOR STRESS

If stress is affecting your behavior and health, then consider trying meditation, which science has proven to relieve stress. When I first began studying meditation, I was surprised to learn that as little as 10 minutes of daily practice can help improve my health and well-being.

My teacher then explained to me that the most important thing is the frequency of meditation, not the length. So, it's more helpful to meditate daily for ten minutes than for an hour weekly.

I integrated that into my routine and later became extremely good at meditating. Now, it's just like any other thing I do automatically every day. And I have also been teaching others how to integrate meditation into their everyday life successfully.

Meditation is popular as a treatment for stress and other mental health challenges. It allows you to enter a deep state of relaxation while becoming more aware of your thoughts and surroundings. You can alleviate chronic stress by meditating for just eight weeks, which science has proven.

The best thing about meditation is that it isn't just a treatment for mental health problems but also a way to bring out your best qualities. That's why you shouldn't just apply the exercise for occasional stress or anxiety relief but also make it a part of your lifetime self-care routine. It will help you become a healthy, compassionate person capable of forming deep, meaningful connections.

Guided meditation will help:

- Make your mind more focused and stable
- Increase your experience of positive emotions
- Increase your ability to open up yourself and connect with others
- Help you let go of regrets about the past and worries about the future and immerse yourself in the present moment

You can practice meditation at any time of the day, but I have found that the best time is when you wake up or right before you go to bed. Meditating right before bedtime helps me sleep more deeply and soundly.

Meditating isn't to eliminate stress – you can't do that – it's to manage it. Meditation teaches you to observe your mental patterns, isolate them, and be less physically and emotionally affected by them. It helps you change your perception of stress and, by effect, your reaction to it.

Stress creates negative stories in the mind. If you allow yourself to get caught up in those stories, you'll keep yourself in the cycle, ensuring that you feel that way for far longer than necessary.

Meditating creates curiosity about your thoughts and feelings, as though you're examining stress from a new perspective. In other words, you deliberately reframe your experience of stress and how you react to it.

Your perception of stress can either aggravate or minimize your physical and emotional responses. With meditation, you learn to step back and observe how your mind fuels stress-inducing thoughts and narratives.

So how do you meditate?

Generally, meditation requires calming your mind and body, quieting your senses, and turning inward to get in touch with who you are beneath the negative thoughts and feelings, and worries of daily life. You can make meditation sessions as short as 10 minutes, but here are the steps involved.

1. **Posture**: Your posture is extremely vital to meditation. Sit upright in a cross-legged pose on the floor or in a chair with your feet flat on the floor. You can place your hands flat on your knees and purse your lips to open your mouth slightly.
2. **Breathe**: Practice the diaphragmatic breathing technique to stabilize your mind. Focus on the rise and fall of your belly or the air passing in and out of your nose.
3. **Motivation**: Find motivation for your meditative exercise. Your motivation may be to address a mental problem you're struggling with.
4. **Release your thoughts**: Meditation practice stresses the importance of letting your thoughts go. This means allowing your thoughts to float naturally without suppressing, ignoring, or paying attention to them. This is how you attune with the deeper part of yourself.

5. **Gratitude**: At the end of your meditation, think about the kindness you've experienced from the universe, family, friends, and strangers. End your session with gratitude.

Distractions come easily during a meditation exercise, especially for beginners. So, it's best to practice guided meditation. You can find guided meditation audios on YouTube, Headspace, and apps made specifically for meditation. And you can use the audio to create your version of guided meditation that applies to your situation.

TAKING A MORE MINDFUL APPROACH

Mindfulness is about grounding yourself in the present moment. It's about taking deep breaths and becoming aware of your thoughts and feelings. By doing this, you will learn more about your body's needs. Being mindful means sitting with an uncomfortable situation for a while instead of reacting to it immediately. This allows your mind and body to cultivate inner strength so that stressors no longer affect you strongly.

These practices will help you take a more mindful approach to daily living.

1. Mindful wakeup

Begin each day with a purpose. Set an intention to make your words, responses, and actions more mindful and compassionate every day. The first thing you should do in the morning is sit in your bed, close your eyes, and tune in to your physical sensations. Then, take three long, deep breaths – in through the nose and out through the mouth. Let your breathing fall into a rhythm as you focus on the rise and fall of your belly.

Ask yourself: "What is my purpose for today?" or "What do I need to feel more connected and fulfilled today?" Then, set your intention – for example, "I will be kind to myself; be generous with my words and actions; be patient with others; remain grounded in the moment," or anything else that matters to you.

Check in with yourself as you go through your day. Pause, breathe, and remember your intention. As you practice this each day, you'll notice a shift in the quality of your mood, communications, and relationships.

2. Mindful eating

Eating can be much more than that bland sensation of "bite, chew, and swallow." Most times, we eat without paying attention to the activity itself. You can make eating a richer and more pleasurable experience by engaging in it mindfully. When you eat, don't do anything else. Focus on the food and how it interacts with your sense of taste and smell. Be in touch with your hunger to avoid eating more than necessary.

3. Mindful walking

Walking can be more than what it is if you take a more mindful approach. Mindful walking means being aware of every step you take and your breathing as you walk. You can practice it anywhere, whether in nature, in the comfort of your home, or at work.

To walk mindfully, focus on the point in front of your feet. Begin by walking slower and more meaningfully than usual. Pay attention to the sensations in your feet as you touch the ground and lift it again. The goal is to pay attention to how you walk, so do just that. Then, shift your attention to whatever you're experiencing in the present moment. Do not engage with it; acknowledge it and let it go.

4. Mindful movement

This involves practicing Yoga techniques to reduce stress. Techniques like child's pose, forward bend, and legs up-the-wall can help with stress relief and gentle body stretching. The different poses can be practiced in the mornings and evenings for relaxation.

Additionally, it helps to quit multitasking – it affects your ability to do things mindfully. Other ways to promote a mindful approach include:

- Body scans
- Listening to relaxing music
- Play

The goal is to create a lifestyle of healthy habits that reduce stress and its effects. I advise starting only some of these strategies at a time, as it may cause stress. However, to make lasting change, starting with one strategy for 10-15 minutes daily is best to cultivate a habit. For example, try 10 minutes of guided meditation when you wake up and PMR before bed. Then, rotate the activities until you successfully integrate them into your daily life.

Of course, for many, chronic stress has taken a toll to the point where it has developed into anxiety and depression. So, in the next chapter, we will discuss how you can take control of anxiety and depression by learning more about triggers and emotional regulation.

Chapter Four Highlights

- Stress is a non-negotiable part of life. It is your body's response to change. But left unchecked, stress leads to anxiety, depression, and other mental health problems. You may not be able to get rid of stress, but you can control and learn to tolerate it.
- The stress response signals you to pay attention to something or take action about a situation as soon as possible. You have to be in tune with this response at all times. Otherwise, you risk getting stuck in fight-or-flight mode, leading to chronic stress or anxiety.
- Stress symptoms affect your thoughts, feelings, behavior, and body as a whole. Knowing your stress symptoms is part of staying in tune with the stress response. You can manage stress by learning to cope with the signs effectively.
- Diaphragmatic breathing is an excellent technique to manage your stress response and symptoms. It can help

with any condition connected to breathing, including stress, anxiety, COPD, asthma, etc. Practice the recommended breathing exercise for at least 10 minutes daily.

- Mindfulness can help you learn more about your body and its needs. It teaches you to stay in the moment and tune with your thoughts and feelings. Practice mindfulness daily to cultivate inner strength and break the power stressors have over you.

TAKING CONTROL OF ANXIETY AND DEPRESSION

Anxiety is one of the most common mental health conditions. It is connected with many disorders; surveys reveal that a third of people have experienced anxiety at some point in their lives.

I have also dealt with anxiety in the past. I know that it is a feeling of fear and distress. However, I did not know then that anxiety is the body's response to stress. You experience anxiety when your body struggles with chronic stress, danger, or a threat.

This response is normal for everyone. But anxiety becomes a disorder when it's present at all times or if it starts interfering with everyday functioning. If left unchecked, anxiety can lead to major depression. This chapter discusses the link between stress, anxiety, and depression.

Many people are unaware, but approximately 121 million people globally suffer from depression. This may seem like an insignificant number when you consider the global population. However, according to statistics, a yearly 850 000 deaths are linked to depression. As the world improves at discussing mental health disorders, we all must become more aware of the consequences to reduce this heartbreaking number.

Before I explain the link between anxiety and depression, let's first look at the difference and similarities between stress and anxiety.

STRESS VS. ANXIETY

Stress and anxiety are both normal responses, but they sometimes overwhelm us. Like stress, anxiety is a natural part of the body's "fight or flight" response – a way of reacting to perceived danger. As noted, this response's purpose is to ensure you're alert, focused, and prepared to deal with any perceived threat.

As I explained in the previous chapter, external factors primarily trigger stress. The trigger could be anything, from work to family or illness. Stress is typically short-term unless it becomes chronic. Once you resolve the source of your stress – like a work issue, for example – it naturally disappears.

On the other hand, anxiety is when the source of stress has been resolved, but the feelings of fear and unease persist. In other words, it is your body's response to stress. You may recognize the unease, distress, or dread you experience before significant events. That feeling is there to help you stay alert, focused, and aware.

The anxiety response can be helpful because it kicks in when you face a physical or emotional threat, real or perceived. However, for many people, it interferes with their daily life.

Stress and anxiety have many similar symptoms. When you're anxious, you might experience the following:

- Increased heart rate
- Faster breathing
- A feeling of dread or worry
- Sweating
- Nervousness
- Restlessness
- Tense muscles
- Diarrhea or constipation

Since stress and anxiety are part of the same response, which makes them have similar symptoms, it can be challenging to distinguish them from each other. As a result, you might be unable to tell when you're experiencing stress or anxiety.

Anxiety manifests differently in people and therefore has varying patterns. When present all the time, it is referred to as Generalized Anxiety, which is different from anxiety or panic attacks – described as intense bouts of anxiety, usually without an observable trigger. But some people also deal with phobias – where specific situations trigger their anxiety. For example, some people have a fear of heights.

I mentioned earlier that anxiety is common in many mental health disorders. It is a hallmark feature of Obsessive-Compulsive Disorder, Post Traumatic Stress Disorder, and other conditions. Individuals suffering from depression often deal with regular bouts of anxiety, and as you've learned, anxiety can cause depression.

It's difficult to pinpoint a specific cause of anxiety. However, many seem to lean towards it due to childhood upbringing and family history. Some research has also indicated that there might be a genetic element to how we experience anxiety.

For many, a life experience of an anxiety-triggering event may lead to the development of an anxiety disorder. Also, some report that a distressing event triggered their first anxiety episode, but then it was followed by other episodes to the point where the disorder appeared to sneak into their lives on its own.

Some common physical and mental symptoms of generalized anxiety include:

- Sleeping troubles
- Incessant worrying
- Feeling stressed and irritable
- Inability to focus, forgetting things
- Poor appetite
- Muscle pains
- Shaking
- Dizziness

Some common symptoms of anxiety attacks:

- Happen suddenly and come on intensely
- A feeling of losing control
- A crippling sense of fear or dread
- Sudden trigger of the physical symptoms highlighted earlier

You experience anxiety when exposed to the trigger event for phobias, but the feelings reduce at other times. Also, you feel compelled to avoid the anxiety-triggering situation.

There are risk factors for anxiety disorders, and they can vary. For example, women are the prominent demographic for generalized anxiety disorder and phobias. In contrast, men and women are equally affected by social anxiety.

But, in general, some risk factors for all types of anxiety disorders include:

- Specific personality traits include being shy when meeting new people or withdrawing in new situations.
- Traumatic experiences in early life or adulthood.
- A family history of mental health disorders such as anxiety.
- Certain physical health conditions, such as arrhythmia or thyroid problems.

UNDERSTANDING ANXIETY TRIGGERS

In the past, when I suffered from anxiety, I sometimes knew what set me off, and other times, I didn't. There were days when my panic seemed to appear out of nowhere. This particular problem made me struggle. How could I hope to manage my anxiety successfully if I couldn't identify the triggers? It's important to know what ticks your anxiety off. Being aware of this is necessary for effective anxiety management.

Science suggests that anxiety is caused by genetics and environmental factors. Many events, situations, and emotions we experience daily may trigger anxiety symptoms or amplify them. These are the things that we refer to as triggers.

Anxiety triggers vary from individual to individual, but people who suffer from anxiety disorders generally experience the same triggers. Most people have numerous triggers. But for some, anxiety can be set off without an obvious trigger.

For these reasons, you must unravel your anxiety triggers. Being able to identify them is the foundation for managing anxiety symptoms successfully.

One thing I learned was that my anxiety largely depended on the type of anxiety I suffered from and the stressors in my daily life. In some cases, knowing the type of anxiety you suffer is key to identifying your triggers.

And in other cases, it's vice versa: identifying your triggers is all you need to determine the type of anxiety you struggle with.

If, for instance, taking the bus makes you incredibly anxious, you may have a phobia or agoraphobia. However, if your anxiety is more of a persistent, low-level feeling of unease or worry, that may be a generalized anxiety disorder.

You might think that you have no anxiety triggers and that your anxiety comes out of nowhere – but this is rarely the case. Unfortunately, a lack of self-awareness usually drowns out the events or emotions that precede anxiety in many cases.

For example, you may be unaware of the connection between the caffeine you drank last night and the heart-racing, dreadful feeling you're experiencing today. That's right – caffeine triggers anxiety in many people.

If you struggle with anxiety, triggers may include life events, habits, and other stressors that seem out of control.

Tracking your anxiety is important if you want to be able to identify triggers. When you feel dread or panicky feelings sneaking up on you, note how you feel and write down what may have preceded that feeling. I started doing this when I learned how to use CBT to tackle my negative feelings. It helped me recognize patterns and think more critically about the elements driving my panic and worry.

On that note, let's talk about common anxiety triggers that I became aware of in my quest to unravel and take control of anxiety.

1. **Physical health issues:** Health issues can be difficult and upsetting. A diagnosis of a chronic illness such as

cancer may trigger or amplify anxiety symptoms. Health problems are powerful triggers because they evoke immediate and personal feelings.

2. **Medications:** Some over-the-counter and prescription medications may trigger anxiety in certain people due to their active ingredients. Many of these ingredients can cause unease or make you unwell, setting off a series of negative thoughts in your mind. But, of course, that only intensifies the symptoms of anxiety. Examples of medications that trigger anxiety are birth control pills, weight loss pills, and cough medications.

3. **Caffeine:** Many people are addicted to caffeine and don't know it. A 2022 review reveals that drinking five cups of coffee daily can increase anxiety and induce panic attacks in individuals with panic disorders. If you need that morning cup of joe to wake up, you might unknowingly trigger or worsen anxiety.

4. **Financial troubles:** Being in debt or worrying about money can make you anxious. Money fears are real, and they can trigger anxiety, too. Additionally, paying an unexpected bill can also induce anxiety in many people. You might need professional help from a financial advisor or a guide to coping with this particular anxiety trigger. A feeling of companionship in the financial process may help you handle the unease better.

5. **Social events:** Many don't find parties or rooms full of strangers fun. And for some, that can induce anxiety. This is referred to as social anxiety disorder. If social events that require interacting with people and making

small talk make you feel uneasy or unwell, you might be dealing with social anxiety disorder.

6. **Conflict:** Disagreements, arguments, and relationship problems are examples of conflicts that can trigger or worsen anxiety. If you find that arguments and disagreements particularly trigger you, learning effective conflict resolution strategies may be the solution to controlling your anxiety.

7. **Stress**: As you've learned, stress is the precursor to anxiety for most people. Everyday stressors such as getting stuck in traffic or missing an appointment can cause anxiety. Stress can make us skip meals, drink more coffee, or miss bedtime – and these factors can also trigger or compound anxiety. Chronic stress is also known to trigger long-term anxiety, worsen symptoms, and cause other health problems.

8. **Public speaking:** Having to speak at public events, partaking in a competition, talking in front of a superior, or even reading aloud in public can lead to anxiety. If your job requires public speaking or performances, you might struggle daily with anxiety.

9. **Negative thinking:** Unpleasant thoughts evoke unpleasant feelings, and that is especially true for anxiety. The thoughts in your head and the words you speak to yourself can trigger anxiety if they are negative. Likewise, language might influence your feelings if you tend to think negatively.

10. **Personal triggers:** These are anxiety triggers that are specific to you and your situation. They are more difficult to identify, but you can work with a trained

psychotherapist to figure them out. Personal triggers may begin with a location, a smell, a song, or even a taste. They consciously or unconsciously remind you of past traumatic events or bad memories.

Other anxiety triggers to watch out for include:

- Lack of sleep
- Substance or alcohol abuse
- Isolation
- Excessive screen time
- Fears and phobias
- Worrying about the future

Here is a detailed list of potential anxiety triggers. Rank them on a scale of 1-10 to determine how anxious these triggers make you feel.

0	1	2	3	4	5	6	7	8	9	10

CALM   **SLIGHTLY ANXIOUS**   **ANXIOUS**   **INTENSELY ANXIOUS**

- Meeting new people
- Relationship conflict or drama
- Going to new places for the first time
- Speaking to a group of people
- Performing in front of many people
- Interacting online
- Unavoidable confrontation
- Texting people on social media

- Having to complete so many tasks
- Communicating with peers or adults
- Working in a team or group
- Having to change your routine
- Leaving your phone unattended for a long time
- Stress from grades or schoolwork
- Raised voices or loud noises
- Being by yourself for a long time
- Giving a presentation in front of your coworkers
- Disappointing friends or family members
- Pressure to behave in specific ways
- Interacting with a crush
- Having too many responsibilities
- Changes in your weight or appearance
- Not being able to pay your bills
- Uncertainty about the future
- Being in tight spaces
- Being in open, public spaces
- Being around some people
- Having to make an important decision

Think about other things that make you anxious and use the scale to rate your anxiety levels.

CBT STRATEGIES FOR ANXIETY

Any strategy that helps you cope with stress successfully can help with anxiety too. Remember the stress management techniques we discussed in the previous chapter? They are also effective for dealing with anxiety. You can also handle anxiety by challenging and reframing your negative thinking patterns using the steps highlighted in Chapter Three.

Other than these, there are specific CBT techniques to better manage your anxiety or anxiety disorder. Let's look at four important ones below.

Journaling for Anxiety

Keeping a journal may seem like something you do as a child or teenager, but there are physical and mental health benefits to journaling in adulthood. Writing is an excellent way to lay out the thoughts in your head. I find that it helps me reflect and fish out patterns in places that I ordinarily wouldn't.

If you're wondering, "Will journaling help me deal with my anxiety?" The answer is yes. The purpose of journaling is to reduce feelings of distress and anxiety and increase your well-being. Not only is it a straightforward technique, but it is also enjoyable. I would go as far as saying it is the CBT technique I find engaging the most.

There are different ways to journal and hardly any limitations on who can do it or benefit from it. You can make it a daily, weekly, or monthly task or do it on an as-needed basis when you feel overwhelmed with stress or anxiety. Choose the journaling method that you think would be most effective for you.

Anxiety left unchecked leads to rumination. But journaling can help you minimize this – it is a powerful technique for examining and reframing your thinking patterns from ruminative to focused and action-oriented.

Another thing journaling is excellent at is helping to monitor stress and anxiety symptoms. It is my favorite way to record my experiences and determine the proper steps toward improving my mental health and relieving anxiety.

Suppose you haven't been able to successfully narrow down the root cause of your anxiety or the feelings it evokes. In that case, keeping a journal is quite effective. It's a good way to identify patterns and possible stressors.

Also, understand that journaling feels different for everyone. We all experience anxiety differently, so it makes sense that we would also journal it differently. I usually stop at a few paragraphs when I journal, but it's okay if you want to write down pages and pages of your thoughts. Just let everything out as it comes.

So, here are the steps I follow:

1. **Write down your thoughts, feelings, and worries:** Start by writing for at least five minutes. Write down whatever you have on your mind, and continue until you feel like you have written enough without developing into rumination. Be as descriptive as possible when writing about specific events causing difficulties in the present. Remember that with anxiety, it's not always about what is presently happening that causes stress, but also worries about what could happen.

2. **Read and reflect:** Review what you have in front of you once you're done writing. Reflect on your thoughts and

feelings, and explore possible options. Could you do anything to change or improve your situation – or your thoughts about the situation? Could things improve for the best? For example, how likely will it happen if you have a particular worry? Can you be sure? If your worry turns out to be true, could you put a spin on it and make it more of a neutral or positive experience rather than a negative one? Is there a way to get a better outcome?

3. **Reframe your thinking:** For every fear or concern in your journal, write down at least one alternative to see it from a different perspective. Create a new narrative and a new set of possibilities. Then, write them down next to the fears and concerns you have. You could also examine cognitive errors to see how you can benefit from reframing anxiety-inducing thinking patterns.

4. **Create a plan:**It helps prepare you for the possibility of your fear getting realized. So if it did happen, what would be your first step? You don't need to have a complete plan; you can jot down steps that you would take and the resources you'd need. Creating a plan will minimize whatever fear you have about the unknown.

Ultimately, it always helps to choose one thing you could do right now to prepare your mind for the future. For instance, you could develop the necessary skills to help you deal with the challenge. Or you could continue to work on your stress and anxiety management skills to increase your emotional resilience.

Role-Playing

With role-playing, you learn new behaviors to help overcome your phobia. In therapy, this is one of the most effective treatments for phobia patients, who usually believe that the situation they fear is dangerous by default – even if it isn't. Unfortunately, this is not a strategy you can do on your own because it involves a patient and a therapist acting out difficult scenarios that the phobia patient fears.

Therapists believe that phobias are caused primarily by learned behaviors and environmental triggers. They believe that phobias are ultimately learned responses to stimuli. Role-playing helps to "unlearn" your response and substitute it with a more rational one, effectively curing the phobia.

In a role-playing session, your therapist assumes the role of that thing you fear, such as a boss or parent. You then interact with them, using behaviors previously learned in therapy. At the end of a role-playing session, there is always a debriefing in which you and your therapist discuss the interaction and find new ways to improve it. This technique will be particularly helpful if you struggle with social or interpersonal phobias.

Essentially, role-playing can help work through learned behaviors in potentially distressing situations. It can lessen your fear and help:

- Improve problem-solving skills
- Gain confidence and familiarity in specific situations
- Acquire better social skills

- Increase assertiveness
- Improve communication skills

Successive Approximation

This aims to help you learn how to tackle challenging goals. This is when you break down complicated or overwhelming tasks into smaller, more practical steps to make them easier to complete. One successive step builds on the previous step, and it helps to gain more confidence as you progress, bit by bit.

For example, suppose you're anxious about a meeting at work. In that case, you can begin by preparing – fire up your laptop, open up the report you need for the meeting, etc. Once you complete these seemingly small tasks, you can progress to other things.

Build upon each task with a bigger one. Each completed task will make you feel like you have a "win" before the big task itself.

Exposure Therapy

Like role-playing, exposure therapy is used specifically to treat phobias. It helps you to confront your fears and phobias. It involves being gradually exposed to your anxiety triggers while your therapist offers guidance on the best way to handle them. This should be done gradually in small increments. Eventually, you should feel more confident and less vulnerable in coping with the things that provoke anxiety.

Exposure therapy is based on the idea of making fear "extinct." When you force yourself to confront a specific fear for a sufficient period, your mind eventually adapts to the stimulus that triggers that fear until it stops evoking stress altogether.

Let's say you have a fear of something ridiculous, like shoes. Pretend you're deathly afraid of shoes to the point where you avoid them entirely and go everywhere barefoot.

Imagine your therapist locks you in a room with one pair of shoes, and there is no way out. At first, you'd be scared; terrified even – the situation would induce a strong anxiety response. But, after maybe 30 minutes, your mind will begin to adapt when nothing happens. You'll eventually get used to being around the pair of shoes, and it will stop inducing fear and anxiety.

How does that happen?

The human brain does not enjoy being under stress. And so, if no danger occurs by being around the thing that causes you to fear, your brain purposely reduces the stress by decreasing the feeling of anxiety it is experiencing by being around the stimulus.

That is how you can use exposure therapy to extinct anxiety by slowly introducing you to a feared stimulus until it no longer makes you afraid.

THE DEPTHS OF DEPRESSION

Depression is an intense sadness accompanied by other symptoms affecting how you think, feel, and behave. It can make you lose interest in activities that once brought you joy. If left unchecked, depression can cause various emotional and physical problems. It can even impair your functioning in your everyday routine, both at work and at home.

Since the brain is such a complex organ, we cannot simply say that depression results from chemical imbalances in the brain. But, sometimes, it is your brain's way of regulating moods, specifically if caused by chronic stress.

The symptoms of depression vary from mild to severe and are as follows:

- An intense or crippling sense of sadness
- Loss of pleasure or interest in favored activities
- Fluctuations in appetite and, by effect, weight
- Sleeping too much or not getting enough sleep
- Loss of energy and rise in fatigue
- Slowed movements and speech
- Feelings of guilt and worthlessness
- Inability to think, concentrate or make decisions
- Thinking about death or suicide

To be diagnosed with depression or major depressive disorder, these symptoms must last at least 14 days, and there must be an observable change in your usual level of functioning.

We often confuse depression with sadness or grief. Loss is a harrowing experience. It can be difficult to endure a loss – of a job, a relationship, or a loved one. In situations like this, it is normal to have feelings of sadness or grief in response. So, we might describe ourselves as being "depressed." But depression is much more than sadness, even though it involves intense sadness.

Anyone can suffer from depression – even those who appear to live a relatively ideal life. Genetics, personality, environmental factors, and biochemistry are typically significant factors that influence the severity of one's depression.

HOW TO START LIFTING YOUR DEPRESSION

First, I'd like you to know that stress and anxiety management techniques such as journaling and cognitive reframing are just as effective for depression. With that said, you can use the following CBT techniques to deal with depression.

- **ABC Analysis**

This method is similar to journaling. However, it focuses on helping you break down behaviors associated with depression, like withdrawing from people or sleeping all the time. The ABC model follows the structure below:

1. First, you analyze the "activating" event, i.e., the trigger.
2. Second, you analyze your "beliefs" about the event. In short, how does the trigger make you feel? And what do you think about it?
3. Third, you analyze the "consequences" of the trigger, including how you feel about it and your behaviors in response to it.

By analyzing triggers and consequences, you can explore possible outcomes and try to explore the underlying causes of your depressive events.

- **Fact-checking**

Fact-checking can help you recognize which behavioral responses are based on emotions or opinions rather than facts. This technique is similar to challenging negative thoughts. It encourages you to challenge your thoughts and understand that they are not rooted in facts. Rather, they are opinions based on your emotions because you're stuck in a harmful thinking pattern.

- **Behavioral experiments**

If your depression is caused by fear and anxiety, you can conduct behavioral experiments in which you imagine the worst possible outcome for a scenario. Then, let this scenario play out in your head to recognize that you can manage any outcome, even if your worst fears come to pass.

To test your behavioral responses to a thought, you can explore the possible outcomes that different thoughts can produce. For example, you can test the thought, "If I am kinder to myself, it will motivate me to work harder," versus "If I harshly criticize myself, it will motivate me to work harder."

Start using criticisms when you need to work harder on something and write down the results. Also, when practicing using kindness and self-compassion, track your results by writing them down. Next, compare the results to see which statement is more accurate.

Behavioral experiments can help test beliefs to determine how to become your best self.

- **Behavioral activation**

This has proved to be an effective treatment for depression. This is when you use certain behaviors to influence your emotional state. For example, losing interest in activities you once enjoyed can intensify depressive symptoms. Still, you can counter that with this technique.

You can activate a positive emotional state by deliberately engaging in specific behaviors – even if you don't feel up to it. So, engage in fulfilling and healthy activities that make you feel good even if you suffer from depression. That will make you more likely to keep participating in meaningful activities that boost your self-worth and self-confidence.

For example, suppose you like playing the keyboard. In that case, depression may cause you to struggle with motivation for playing. As a result, you may stop playing altogether, unknowingly reinforcing the feeling of hopelessness and depriving yourself of an activity that makes you feel good about yourself.

However, if you push yourself to play the keyboard for just five minutes daily, you prove to yourself that you still got it. That can improve your mood, keep you active, and remind you of the things that make you happy.

- **Writing self-statements to counter negative thoughts**

When you notice negative thoughts plaguing you, counteract them by writing down the opposite of that thought – specifically something positive. This method may be difficult if you're a CBT newbie, but it is also extremely effective. So, it's worth trying out, no matter what.

For example, if a negative thought like, "I am a failure," keeps popping into your head, write down something like, "I am a person with great potential," or "I have great prospects." Of course, it might be difficult to replace dysfunctional thoughts initially. Still, the more you practice, the easier it will be to create an association with those positive self-statements.

Journaling is challenging for everyone, so I have developed five prompts to help you start writing and expressing your thoughts and feelings. Choose one from below.

1. What is a situation that made me sad today?
2. What feeling is most dominant today? Which part of my body is it concentrated in? What emotion would I like to replace it with?
3. When I have the energy, what would I like to do?
4. If I could change something in my life right now, what would it be? How can I start working on making that change?
5. My inner critic needs to quiet down because ...

Please see a professional immediately if you struggle with severe depression and suicidal thoughts.

As I have established, stress, anxiety, and depression all have physical symptoms. But when the body cannot cope with a perceived threat, these physical symptoms can become panic attacks. The next chapter will explore what it feels like to experience panic attacks and how you can cope.

Chapter Five Highlights

- Anxiety is the cumulative result of persistent, unresolved stress. Just as stress is the body's response to change, anxiety is the body's response to stress. It is a nagging feeling of fear and unease that arises to help you stay alert and focused before a significant event. Anxiety isn't inherently harmful, but your reaction to it can be.
- Anxiety triggers are different for everyone. Anything can be an anxiety trigger. Changing how you react to

anxiety begins by figuring out your triggers. Self-awareness is the foundation for tracking anxiety triggers.

- CBT techniques can help you manage anxiety by tracking and reframing negative thought patterns, which change how you react to them. You can also cope with anxiety better using the stress management techniques recommended in the previous chapter.
- Depression is often confused with sadness or grief, but they are different emotions. Depression can impair functioning and cause various physical and mental health problems. However, you may be able to fight depression by tackling chronic stress or anxiety.
- Journaling, cognitive reframing, and other CBT anxiety management techniques also work effectively for depression.

ALTRUISM

"Altruism is the best source of happiness. There is no doubt about that"

— DALAI LAMA

Did you know that people who help others without expecting anything in return usually get what they give in 100 folds? They live longer and enjoy the good things in life. In this journey of ours, I'd like to create an opportunity where you can help a complete stranger.

So, would you like to make an impact in this world? You may wonder, "How can I do this?" The reality is that there are people out there similar to you, who have less exposure, and are currently searching for information but don't know where to find it. You can be that beacon of light by pointing them in the right direction and contributing to changing their lives.

The only way I can also accomplish my purpose of helping others is by informing them about this book. And as we already know, most people judge a book by not only its cover, but by the quality of the reviews.

If you've found this book helpful, can you take a moment and let other potential readers know about your experience? Even though sharing an honest review should take less than one minute, it's your own way of impacting the lives of others.

Your review will help save the lives of people whose assumptions have taken control of their lives and who are on the verge of losing a loved one, a partner, a dream job, a marriage, a relationship, and their purpose of living.

One life changed means you're contributing to the good of humanity – please let's do this.

Now, it's time to act!

If you're reading this book on Kindle or a tablet, simply scroll down to the review section and click on the prompt to leave a review.

If you are using Audible, click on the three grey dots to the right of your purchase, and you'll see a prompt that says "Rate and Review." Remember, a few sentences of your experience can change someone's life.

If you feel good about helping strangers you don't know, thank you! The world needs more people like you.

I hope you're as excited as I am for the coming chapters because I'll be covering some constructive topics.

Your review means the world to me and others; thank you. Now let's go back and continue from where we were.

- Your number one supporter, R.J. Miller.

HOW TO COPE WITH PANIC ATTACKS

> *"A panic attack goes from 0 to 100 in an instant. It's halfway between feeling like you'll faint and feeling like you'll die"*

— UNKNOWN

Have you ever experienced an episode of intense anxiety that lasted quite briefly but had you feeling like your world was ending or your chest was closing in on itself? If yes, you're familiar with panic attacks. However, even if you've never experienced one personally, you have probably watched a TV or movie character go through that brief episode.

A panic attack is a sudden and brief episode of intense fear and anxiety that triggers strong physical sensations and reactions without an external cause or real danger. It is the same as anxiety but crippling on an entirely new level. Physical signs of a panic attack may include increased heart rate, shortness of breath, trembling, dizziness, and muscle tension.

Panic attacks are often unexpected and usually unrelated to a visible external threat. They occur quite frequently and can last up to half an hour. However, the effects of a panic attack last for a few hours. And for someone who experiences them regularly, the effects can last a lifetime.

Many people have experienced one or two attacks in their lifetime, which tend to go away, usually when the source of stress ends. According to available data, approximately 35% of the American population experience panic attacks at one point in their lives. That is how common they are. Panic attacks are also referred to as anxiety attacks.

I have never had an anxiety attack, but I have witnessed a few episodes of friends who struggle with them. The experience can be frightening. When a panic attack happens, a victim might think that they're having a heart attack or dying, feeling that they are losing control. However, for many, the crippling feelings of panic only arise during periods of stress or illness.

If you experience recurring episodes of anxiety attacks, that means you have a panic disorder – which, as you've learned, is a type of anxiety disorder. People with panic disorders generally have unexpected and recurring anxiety attacks and a never-ending fear of repeated episodes.

But panic attacks aren't always caused by anxiety. Some symptoms of panic attacks are associated with some medical conditions. Certain medications and drugs, including caffeine, alcohol, and tranquilizers, also induce symptoms of panic attacks.

A panic disorder isn't life-threatening, but it can significantly affect a person's quality of life. Unless you learn to control them or seek treatment, prolonged panic attacks can severely destabilize your life. You may even be forced to avoid going outside or being alone for fear of having an attack.

Symptoms of Panic attacks

A panic attack typically happens without warning. It can attack at any time – when you're in the middle of a presentation, driving home, at the mall, or even sound asleep while having a beautiful dream.

Panic attacks vary, but the symptoms peak within minutes. A panic attack's aftermath may leave you tired and worn out.

When an anxiety attack begins, you may experience some of these symptoms or reactions:

- Fear of loss of control
- Fear of death
- Tightness in the throat
- Shortness of breath
- Rapid heartbeats
- Trembling
- Headache
- Chest pain
- Nausea

- Numbness
- Cold or chills
- A feeling of detachment from reality

Perhaps the worst thing about having a panic attack is the crippling fear of a repeated attack. I mentioned earlier that a panic attack is the same as anxiety and can be triggered during periods of stress. Does that mean it has a connection to the body's fight-or-flight-or-freeze response? You are about to find out.

GETTING ACQUAINTED WITH THE FIGHT, FLIGHT, OR FREEZE RESPONSE

I explained a few chapters back that the fight-flight-freeze response is how your body naturally reacts to danger, which may or may not be real. It is a stress response to prepare you for perceived threats, such as a lurking shadow in the dark streets of your neighborhood or a growling dog.

When the body is threatened or faced with possible danger, the brain instructs the automatic nervous system to activate the 'fight-flight-freeze' response. The activation floods the body with various chemicals, i.e., neurotransmitters, triggering physiological changes.

However, you don't necessarily have to be in real danger for your body to activate this response. This means the response can activate in situations where it isn't needed. This is what triggers panic attacks.

An anxiety attack occurs when this stress response is activated with no real threat or danger in sight. Your body can enter the fight-or-flight mode and induce panic attack symptoms in the most stress-free situations, such as sleeping or watching TV.

People also react to perceived danger differently, which is how the name "fight, flight, or freeze" originated.

The stress response is involuntary and includes some physiological changes that prepare you to:

- Fight – take action to get rid of the threat
- Flight – flee away from the threat
- Freeze – become immobile in the face of the threat

Some include a fourth reaction, "fawn," which involves trying to please the individual representative of the threat to stop them from harming you. We also have a fifth potential reaction: tonic immobility. Some refer to this as a "flop." It is when you become entirely unresponsive, both physically and mentally. For instance, fainting in response to a perceived threat is a "flop" response.

Together, scientists refer to fight-flight-freeze as the acute stress response.

One by one, let's discuss what happens when your body is in fight, flight or freeze mode.

What happens in "fight or flight" mode?

The autonomic nervous system (ANS) is the part of your nervous system in charge of rapid, unconscious responses, including reflexes. For example, when you're faced with a threat, the brain contacts the ANS, which sends the body messages to prepare for danger in a specific way.

If you experience the "fight or flight" response, your body will instantly experience physiological changes such as:

- **Increased heart rate and rapid breathing:** This happens so your body can send more oxygenated blood to your brain and muscles in case you need to escape danger physically. It also triggers a rise in blood pressure.
- **Flushing:** As your body sends blood to vital areas, your skin may become flushed or paler than usual or alternate between flushed and pale.
- **Dry mouth:** The blood vessels around your mouth constrict, causing the salivary glands to halt saliva production, leading to a dry mouth temporarily.
- **Dilated pupils:** Your pupils dilate to make more room for light to enter the eyes. This allows you to see better so that you can observe your environment.
- **Tense muscles:** As your muscles prepare for physical action, they tense up, which can cause trembling or shaking. Tense muscles may also trigger a constriction in the throat, leading to a higher-pitched voice.

In the "fight or flight" state, you may feel severely agitated, alert, or argumentative. Or you may feel like leaving wherever you are. A "fight or flight" response that is more intense than usual can become a panic attack. It can also induce an asthma attack in someone with the condition.

What happens in 'freeze' mode?

The 'freeze' response's physiological process differs from fight or flight. Scientists describe it as a state of "attentive immobility." While you're "frozen," you remain extremely alert but cannot take physical action against the perceived threat.

If you experience the 'freeze' response, you may develop the following:

- Physical immobility
- Muscle tension
- A rapid decline in heart rate

While freezing seems like a counterintuitive response to danger, it has its purpose. First, it prepares you for action. Scientists have observed that it allows animals to scan the environment to decide their next step. When you freeze, your brain uses that time to contemplate the best way to respond to the danger.

Also, freezing enables you to perceive your surroundings better. In a 2015 study, researchers monitored people's reactions to shock and its effect on their ability to process visual information. They found that participants who froze in response to shock better understood poorly defined images and were able to process threat-relevant information more quickly.

In some situations, the 'freeze' response can help you hide. Sometimes, hiding and staying very still keeps you safe from an attack or causes the attacker to lose interest in harming you. In animals, tonic immobility is used as a last resort when "fight or flight" fails since many predators don't eat something dead.

Finally, freezing can cause dissociation, thus reducing the impact of an event. Dissociation occurs when an individual experiences trauma. It makes a person feel detached or numb in the face of a threat, which makes a severely distressing event feel less real. This could be why the freeze response happens more frequently in individuals with a history of trauma.

There is psychological fear when the fight-flight-freeze response triggers physiological reactions without an apparent cause. That fear is conditioned, meaning you've associated an event or thing with negative experiences. This psychological response is activated the first time you're exposed to the situation, after which it develops over time.

We refer to that as a perceived threat – something you consider potentially dangerous. Perceived threats vary from individual to individual. With a phobia, your brain thinks you're in danger because it considers the situation that triggers your phobia to be life-threatening. As a result, your body activates the fight-flight-freeze response to keep you safe.

However, the response can be overactive. Thus, a non-threatening situation can trigger the associated physical reaction.

That is how panic attacks happen – resulting from the activated fight-flight-freeze response.

An overactive stress response is typically more common in individuals who have experienced the following:

Trauma

Some people develop an exaggerated stress response after going through a traumatic event. It involves a repeated pattern of physical reactions linked to the actual event. So, you're more likely to experience panic attacks if you have a history of PTSD, assault, childhood trauma, accidents, natural disasters, or stressful life events.

In this case, your brain activates fight-flight-freeze in response to related triggers to prepare you for future traumatic events. Unfortunately, that can lead to an overactive response, causing panic attacks.

For example, if you've been in a car accident, the sound of a car may remind you of the traumatic event. You might have a panic response from simply hearing a car honking.

Anxiety

As I've established, anxiety is a natural response that helps you respond appropriately to a perceived threat. But if you have an anxiety disorder, you're likely to experience anxiety attacks triggered by non-threatening stressors. For example, you could develop an exaggerated stress response to simple activities, such as sitting in traffic or speaking at a business meeting.

Fortunately, you can learn to cope with an overactive stress response and control your panic attacks. But first, let's discuss why it is essential for you to learn how to control panic attacks.

THE IMPORTANCE OF LEARNING HOW TO CONTROL PANIC ATTACKS

Remember the autonomic nervous system? It has a subsystem known as the sympathetic nervous system: your body's default alarm system. The sympathetic nervous system (SNS) is a harmonized network of nerves, hormones, and brain structures. An imbalanced SNS can cause serious complications.

You learned earlier that the ANS is the body's involuntary response center. Without conscious decisions, the ANS controls vital bodily functions, including heart rate, digestion, blood pressure, body temperature, pupil dilation, etc. This is how we can make quick internal adjustments and external reactions without consciously thinking about it.

However, the sympathetic nervous system is specifically responsible for the stress response. When the SNS activates the involuntary response to a stressful or dangerous situation, it floods the body with hormones that boost alertness, heart rate, etc.

It triggers the physiological reactions of the fight-flight-freeze response, and this happens so quickly that we don't even realize it's happened. For example, you may jump from the path of an oncoming car before fully registering that it is racing toward you.

The sympathetic nervous system activates the stress response but doesn't deactivate it once the perceived threat is eliminated. This is done by the parasympathetic nervous system – another subsystem of the autonomic nervous system.

The parasympathetic nervous system activates the 'rest and digest' to calm the body down after a stressful situation. As a result, heart rate, blood pressure, hormone production, etc., revert to normal levels as the body enters a state of equilibrium, also called homeostasis.

Chronic stress occurs when the body spends too much time in fight-flight-freeze mode and not enough time in 'rest and digest mode. The parasympathetic nervous system activates after a meal or during a pleasurable activity, and the physical effects include:

- Reduced heart rate and respiration
- Drop in blood pressure
- Increase in intestinal activity
- Blood flow to the digestive tract increases
- Cortisol and adrenaline decrease
- Neurotransmitters that regulate muscle contractions increase

Normal body function is achievable only if the sympathetic and parasympathetic nervous systems work harmoniously to maintain the standard baseline.

The SNS controls the body's stress response by interacting with the hypothalamus-pituitary-adrenal (HPA) axis. Stress triggers the secretion of hormones like cortisol, epinephrine, and norepinephrine to increase blood pressure and blood sugar.

As I said, after a stressful event, the parasympathetic nervous system kicks in to decrease the production of the hormones mentioned before and lower blood pressure by releasing neuro-transmitters, including acetylcholine.

It would be an oversimplification to say that the SNS and PNS are antagonistic. Both systems exist to maintain homeostasis throughout the body. To do this, they can work together, against each other, or independently. The key is to maintain balance.

Think of the SNS and the PNS as existing on either side of a scale: each work to counteract the effect of the other. If balanced, the body enters homeostasis and functions as usual. However, this balance can be disrupted by several factors, including disease.

Some physical and mental conditions can make the sympathetic nervous system overactive. This makes it impossible for the parasympathetic nervous system to activate 'rest and digest.' This imbalance underlies mental health problems such as chronic stress, anxiety, depression, and panic attacks.

The SNS' stress response is incredibly useful in short bursts, especially with the boost of mental focus. However, if prolonged, it wreaks havoc on your physical and mental health. Besides keeping you in a constant state of stress, the continuous production of stress hormones like cortisol and epinephrine can increase blood pressure, damage blood vessels, and lead to unhealthy fat accumulation.

Symptoms of an overactive stress response include:

- Anxiety
- Panic attacks
- Insomnia
- Breathlessness
- Poor digestion
- High blood pressure
- High cholesterol
- Palpitations
- Inability to self-soothe or relax

So, while the SNS' stress response serves a purpose, you don't want it overactive or "on" all the time.

Are you stuck in a "fight or flight?"

It is referred to as a sustained sympathetic tone when you're stuck in the "fight or flight" mode. And it can lead to:

- **Fatigue or exhaustion** – You are in a constant state of tiredness. Even though you're eating healthy and taking care of yourself, you still feel like you have no strength or stamina.

- **Poor immune response** – Attention shifts somewhere else in your body, leaving your immune response unsupported and dysfunctional.
- **Slow metabolism** – The digestive system slows down because the blood supply is constantly redirected to your muscles. This makes your resting metabolism suffer.
- **Lack of focus** – When you're stressed and overwhelmed, you tend to forget things.

Being stuck in "fight or flight" can also make you generally unwell. You may become snappy and irritable with the people in your life. You may also experience migraines, dizziness, sleep issues, anxiety, and panic due to being stuck in the "fight or flight" state.

The solution is learning to induce the 'rest and digest response' whenever you feel stressed. This can help you maintain the balance between the sympathetic and parasympathetic nervous systems and reduce stress response activity.

CALMING THE BODY BACK TO A REST AND DIGEST STATE

Panic attacks happen with very little warning, so you should have readily available coping strategies to stop a panic episode as soon as it happens. To do this, you must explore different ways to deactivate the sympathetic nervous system's response and instead seduce the parasympathetic nervous system to take over.

- **Breathing exercise**

It's normal for physical sensations, such as chest tightness and rapid breathing, to become intense and overwhelming during a panic attack. However, a breathing exercise can help you feel calm and relaxed despite the unpleasant physical symptoms.

By directing attention to your breath, you can focus on that instead of fixating on what's happening to you physically. Breathing exercises can also help with hyperventilation and palpitations common in intense anxiety or panic attacks.

Breathe slowly and deeply, focusing on each breath. Gather your breath from your abdomen, filling your lungs slowly as you count to 4 when you inhale or exhale. You can also try the 4-7-8 technique, where you inhale for 4 seconds, hold for 7 seconds, and exhale slowly for 8 seconds.

Note: Breathing exercises can amplify some people's panic attack symptoms. In such a case, you can try the following strategy.

- **Retreat to a peaceful spot away from stimuli**

Stimuli can overwhelm the senses and intensify a panic attack. You can stop a panic attack by finding a calmer and more peaceful spot. For example, if you are in a busy room, leave and find a spot with zero distractions. An alternative is to move to rest against a nearby wall.

Retreating to a calm and quiet place creates mental space, making it easier to practice breathing exercises or try another coping strategy.

- **Focus on one stimulus to drown out others**

Focusing on a physical object in your immediate surroundings can help you feel grounded when you're overwhelmed with distressing physical symptoms. The idea is to drown out other stimuli by focusing on a single stimulus.

Choose a specific item in your environment and focus on it. As you look at the object, you may start to think about its texture, wonder how it was made or who made it, and how it came to be in the room. This can help reduce panic attack symptoms.

If you suffer from recurrent panic attacks, you can carry a familiar object around to help you stay grounded. This could be a tiny toy, a crystal or smooth stone, a seashell, etc.

- **5-4-3-2-1**

Panic attacks can make you dissociate due to the intensity and how it overwhelms your senses. The 5-4-3-2-1 grounding technique helps you reroute your focus away from stressors. You can practice this method by completing the following steps slowly and carefully.

1. Look at 5 different items. Focus on each one for a few minutes.
2. Listen for 4 different sounds. Think about their source and what distinguishes them.
3. Touch 3 separate objects. Think about their texture, temperature, and usage.
4. Sniff 2 different smells. It could be the scent of your soap or brewed coffee.
5. Identify one thing you can taste. You can focus on whatever taste you have in your mouth or taste a piece of candy.

- **Repeat a mantra or an affirmation**

A mantra is a sound, word, or phrase that helps you focus and ground yourself in the present. You can use a mantra to reassure yourself, such as "This too shall pass" or "I am strong, brave, and calm." Or you can try something with a deeper, more spiritual meaning. Repeating a mantra aloud or internally can help you stop a panic attack in its tracks.

Focus on gently repeating the mantra, and your physical responses will start to slow, making it easier to regulate your breathing and relax your body.

Another way to stop a panic attack is to stimulate your vagus nerve – a cranial nerve located on both sides of your voice box. The vagus nerve is the longest cranial nerve and is connected to branches of the parasympathetic nervous system. Therefore, you can induce the PNS' 'rest and digest' response by stimulating the vagus nerve.

You can stimulate the vagus nerve by humming, singing, or chewing gum. This lets the brain know that your body isn't under attack and there's no real or perceived threat. Other ways to stimulate the vagus nerve include massage and cold exposure.

Affirmations to repeat during a panic attack

An affirmation is a positive statement about yourself. Positive affirmations are positive self-talk, meaning you can use them to counter negative thoughts and self-beliefs. You can use self-affirmations to ease stress and anxiety and promote positive life changes. Repeating affirmations can help you stop a panic attack as soon as possible.

Below is a list of affirmations you can repeat during a panic attack. But you can also create unique affirmations by drawing on the things that speak to you. Regardless, the goal is to use affirmations as a healthy tool to manage anxiety attacks.

- "I am in control."
- "This too shall pass."
- "I believe in my strength."
- "I inhale peace and exhale fear."
- "This feeling will pass."
- "I am strong and capable."
- "I am enough."
- "I am safe and protected."
- "I let go and free myself."
- "I will move past this moment."

If you're suffering from an obsessive or addictive behavior, you need a more tailored, hands-on approach to CBT. We will look at the methods you can use in the next chapter.

Chapter Seven Highlights

- Panic attack symptoms vary from individual to individual. Still, the common symptoms are intense anxiety, dizziness, shortness of breath, numbness, sweating, and a racing heart. A panic attack episode might feel like you're dying or having a heart attack.
- Panic attacks aren't dangerous or harmful in themselves. However, they can be a symptom of other severe psychological conditions or health problems. Therefore, you should get a proper diagnosis from a medical expert to determine the specific cause of your attacks.
- You can experience panic attacks with no apparent trigger. An episode can happen suddenly anywhere, any time – driving, during a meeting, or even while sleeping. It's possible to experience one or two panic attack episodes without ever experiencing any after that. It is called a panic disorder if you suffer from recurring panic episodes.
- Avoidance isn't the best tactic for dealing with panic attacks. Don't be tempted to avoid event triggers or social situations. Avoidance only exacerbates your fear. Instead, the best policy is to face your fears head-on using the recommended CBT approach, such as Exposure and Response Prevention therapy.

- Certain CBT techniques can help you treat panic attacks successfully. For example, you can combine stress management methods with other CBT techniques to reduce the frequency and intensity of panic attack episodes. They will also help you cope better when an episode starts to happen.

OVERCOMING OBSESSIVE AND ADDICTIVE BEHAVIORS

One of the scariest things anyone can experience in life is feeling out of control. Unfortunately, this is something that individuals with obsessive behaviors and addiction struggle with daily. Obsessive behavior can look different in people – compulsive gambling, spending, sexual behavior, and behavioral rituals are only a few examples.

Individuals with obsessive-compulsive disorder (OCD) experience never-ending distress due to their obsessions. Yet, they feel compelled to perform any behavior or ritual that provides them temporary relief.

The thing about these types of mental health problems is that you not only struggle with anxiety, depression, and negativity. You also live with guilt, shame, and poor self-worth.

Cognitive behavioral therapy can help you take back control of your life. You don't have to let OCD, substance abuse, chemical dependence, shopping addiction, or any other kind of addiction and other compulsive behaviors rule your life. With cognitive behavioral therapy techniques, you can address problematic thoughts and feelings to overcome obsessive behavior or addiction.

CBT is used widely in treating all types of addictions and obsessive disorders. It teaches you to find connections between your thoughts, feelings, and behaviors to increase awareness of how these three things impact your recovery process.

Alongside addiction, CBT is an effective treatment for co-occurring disorders like:

- Obsessive-compulsive disorder
- Eating disorders
- Bipolar disorders

CBT shows that many harmful thoughts and feelings behind addiction and obsessive behavior are neither rational nor logical. They sometimes stem from negative past experiences or environmental and biological factors.

When an individual struggling with addiction or obsessive behavior understands why they think or feel a certain way and how their thoughts and feelings lead to compulsions or substance use, it becomes easier to overcome their mental health issues.

If you struggle with addiction or OCD, CBT can help you to identify your "automatic negative thoughts." As I've explained, these thoughts originate from impulse and are based on misconceptions and feelings of fear and self-doubt. It's common for people to try to self-medicate intrusive thoughts with substance abuse or behavioral rituals.

Not all obsessive-compulsive behaviors are the same. So, let's first discuss how CBT can address different types of compulsive behavior.

CBT AND OBSESSIVE-COMPULSIVE DISORDER

Obsessive-compulsive disorder involves a pattern of intrusive thoughts, ideas, images, urges, and fears (obsessions) that leads one to perform specific repetitive behaviors (compulsions). Compulsions can be physical rituals, such as hand cleaning or checking on something, or mental rituals, like counting and other activities, which compel you to do something repetitively to eliminate the distressing, unwanted thoughts in your head.

We all have varying degrees of unwanted thoughts and repetitive behaviors, but this doesn't mean we have OCD. For those with OCD, these thoughts are persistently intrusive – they don't go away until you give in and complete the associated compulsion.

Not performing the behavioral ritual causes great distress, usually linked to an intense fear of negative consequences, if one does not complete the behavior. In addition, obsessions and compulsions interfere with the daily functioning of those with OCD and can cause a significant decline in their social interactions.

You may try to fight the obsessions by ignoring the thoughts or ideas inside your head, but that only significantly amplifies your fears and distress. Ultimately, you feel like you have no choice but to perform the compulsive act that will ease your distress.

They only keep coming back despite attempts at ignoring or suppressing the bothersome thoughts or urges. And that leads you to engage in more ritualistic acts – keeping you in a vicious cycle of obsessions and compulsions.

As someone with OCD, you might suspect your thoughts are unrealistic and false. But even if you know they are not realistic or true, you may find it incredibly hard to disengage from the obsessive thoughts or stop the behavioral rituals altogether.

Think of the different forms of OCD as subtypes of obsessive thoughts. Though OCD and compulsive behaviors generally have similar symptoms, they present differently in people. Here are examples of common OCD subtypes:

- **Contamination obsessions:** Fear of contracting germs or diseases and getting sick.
- **Harm obsessions:** Fear of harming self or potentially harming others.
- **Symmetry obsessions:** being fixated on the organization of items.
- **Body-focused compulsions:** Compulsively picking, biting, or pulling at hair, skin, or nails.
- **Relationship obsessions:** Focusing on the "rightness" or uncertainty of intimate relationships.

Anxiety is at the root of obsessive and compulsive behavior. But CBT can help you understand that while the obsession-related anxiety is real, not giving in to the intrusive thoughts won't affect you – even if it feels that way.

CBT strategies for treating OCD act based on the fact that obsessions and compulsions develop and intensify due to deeply ingrained, dysfunctional thought patterns that push an affected person to react to their thoughts and feelings in dysfunctional ways.

CBT aims to teach you to form a new relationship with your thoughts to stop them from maintaining your anxiety. More importantly, it also aims to help you develop a more effective and healthier approach to responding to your obsessions and compulsions. You can also use CBT to identify and challenge the cognitive processes that intensify your OCD symptoms and their associated meanings.

Leaving compulsive behavior unattended can have significant emotional, physical, relational, financial, and legal consequences. Therefore, the sooner you start your recovery process, the greater your chances of success.

There are many highly effective CBT techniques for treating obsessive behaviors, but we will focus on Exposure and Response Prevention. This strategy breaks the bond between automatic negative thoughts and ritualistic compulsive actions. They also train you to stop ritualizing when you feel overwhelmingly anxious.

You can start noticing improvements within weeks of practicing either of these treatment therapies. OCD treatment is typically short-term, but it has lasting benefits. Of course, this depends on how severe your symptoms are.

Exposure and Response Prevention (ERP)

Many therapists argue that this is the most helpful CBT technique for treating OCD. This is because ERP involves exposing yourself to distress-inducing intrusive thoughts without engaging in the compulsive ritual.

The aim is to prevent yourself from getting the temporary relief associated with performing the compulsion, forcing you to face the anxiety until it fades. Eventually, with consistent practice, you become desensitized to obsessive thoughts.

With ERP, the exposure to situations that trigger intrusive thoughts must be gradual and controlled. The symptoms usually become mild to the point where you learn to ignore them; sometimes, they disappear entirely. Over time, you will learn to respond differently to the trigger, causing a significant decline in the intensity of obsessions and frequency of compulsive behaviors.

Below are the steps in practicing exposure and response prevention by yourself.

1. First, write down a detailed description of your triggers, obsessions, and compulsions. Now, rank them

from the most difficult to the least bothersome. After this, begin with the easiest obsession and the symptoms.

2. Put yourself in situations that trigger your obsessions (exposure). During this phase, avoid performing the behavioral ritual for 15-30 minutes (response prevention). Then, with every session, avoid performing the compulsion for longer periods. Soon, you will notice that when you don't perform the ritual, your anxiety increases rapidly, peaks, and then goes downward.

In situations where it is impossible to expose yourself to the actual situation that triggers obsessive thoughts and compulsion, you can use visualization or recordings to practice imagined exposure and effectively increase your anxiety levels for the CBT exercises.

Once the associated anxiety with the least bothersome symptoms decreases significantly or completely fades away, you can take on more challenges until they become manageable. Effective ERP exercises result in "habituation," meaning you learn that nothing bad happens when you don't perform rituals.

For example, suppose you have contamination OCD, i.e., an obsessive fear of contracting germs or disease. In that case, you may start by getting yourself to touch a dusty desk – which you believe may be contaminated – and then wait for at least 20 minutes to wash your hands. Subsequently, you can wait for longer and longer periods before you clean your hands.

Over time, the gradual, repeated exposure and delayed response will condition you to respond differently to the fear of germs, which, in turn, will cause a decrease in the frequency of the obsession.

OVERCOMING ADDICTION WITH CBT

Cognitive behavioral therapy can be life-saving if you struggle with chemical dependence, substance abuse, addiction, or dependence. By teaching you to identify and address negative thought patterns and feelings, CBT can help you overcome addiction.

When an individual with addiction understands the underlying reason behind their feelings or behavior and how it contributes to substance use, it becomes much easier for them to overcome addiction.

I explained early in the book that negative thought patterns are the primary cause of anxiety disorders and depression. It's no coincidence that these conditions typically co-occur with addiction. The presence of negative thinking patterns can make you more likely to abuse alcohol and drugs or develop other kinds of addiction.

As I said, addiction sometimes develops because people try to self-medicate the unpleasant or distressing thoughts and feelings in their heads with drugs or alcohol. CBT can help you defeat addiction by:

- Providing valuable self-help techniques and tools to improve your mood.
- Helping to identify, challenge, and dismiss the inaccurate beliefs and insecurities that contribute to addiction.
- Teaching how to communicate effectively.

CBT also helps you cope with addiction triggers in three key ways:

- Recognize – identify triggers that lead to engaging in addiction (drinking, drug use, shopping)
- Avoid – remove yourself from trigger situations when appropriate and possible.
- Cope – practice CBT exercises to address and neutralize dysfunctional emotions and thoughts contributing to addiction.

CBT for addiction treatment requires you to identify any co-occurring psychological disorders and analyze how addiction negatively impacts your physical, social, emotional, and spiritual development. Understanding the impact is central to getting back on track with recovery.

My favorite thing about CBT for overcoming addiction is that you can work with a therapist to create a personalized treatment plan. You can replace ineffective coping mechanisms with healthy and safe skills.

CBT Addiction Exercises

You can employ specific CBT exercises to overcome addiction such:

- **Recording thought**

This exercise is to help you examine automatic negative thoughts and find objective evidence to challenge, support, or disprove the thoughts. You must record and cross-examine evidence for and against your negative thoughts and assumptions.

Example: "My partner thinks I'm unlovable, and drinking makes me feel better about myself" can be challenged and replaced with *"I can learn how I am unlovable and become a better person. I don't need to drink to feel good about myself."*

- **Behavioral exercise**

This exercise compares dysfunctional thoughts against positive, healthy ones to determine which can effectively alter behavior. For example, self-criticism works for some people, while self-kindness is the best route for others. A behavioral exercise will help you see which approach is best for your recovery process and journey.

Example: "If I criticize myself harshly after drinking heavily, I drink less" versus *"If I practice compassion after drinking heavily, I drink less."*

- **Pleasant activity exercise**

Create a list of healthy and fun activities you can practice daily. There should be enough activities to last a week. Ensure the tasks are easy to complete while evoking positive emotions. The aim is to reduce negative thoughts and, by effect, the need to drink, use drugs, or go on a shopping spree by scheduling pleasurable and enjoyable activities.

Example: When you get the urge to drink or use drugs, use that time to dance to your favorite music.

- **Advantages and Disadvantages**

This is a warm-up exercise to try before starting your CBT recovery journey. Get a journal and write down the advantages and disadvantages of your addictive behavior. For example:

Addictive behavior	Advantages	Disadvantages
Excessive drinking		
Quitting alcohol		
Using drugs		
Quitting drugs		

- **Identify external triggers**

Triggers are those situations that affect your brain and can push you toward an addictive behavior even when you've decided to stop. Therefore, the intention to quit must reflect in your behavior, keeping you away from potential triggers.

So, write down the strongest triggers for you. Then, write down specific triggers that could interfere with your recovery process – at least 20. Your triggers should include people, places, feelings, times, objects, and situations.

- **Thought-stopping technique**

The thought-stopping technique is key to interrupting the *trigger-thought-craving-use* sequence. It helps to disrupt the process. It would help if you stopped the thought as soon as it begins by promptly taking action.

Try this technique in two ways: Visualization and Relaxation. With visualization, imagine a switch in your mind and picture yourself moving the switch from ON to OFF to stop your unhelpful thoughts. Replace the thoughts with something healthier and more positive.

Relaxation involves practicing a breathing exercise. Take a deep breath from the belly and slowly exhale. Do this at least three times. Repeat this whenever your thoughts are triggered.

Note: Cravings last up to 15 minutes, so practice any of these exercises for that long.

- **Identifying internal triggers**

Your internal triggers set off the brain to think about engaging in addictive behavior. Below is a list of feelings and emotions that might trigger thoughts about engaging in addictive behavior. Place a checkmark next to the ones that apply to you.

- Angry
- Frustrated
- Afraid
- Bored
- Jealous
- Nervous
- Insecure
- Criticized
- Sad
- Embarrassed
- Pained
- Irritated
- Hungry
- Worried
- Overwhelmed
- Exhausted
- Lonely
- Excited
- Guilty
- Sleepy
- Envious
- Anxious

Write down other emotional states that trigger you to engage in an addiction. Describe situations where a specific change in mood triggered cravings for an addiction. For example, you argued with someone, got angry, and felt the urge to use it.

Overcoming addiction requires working with a support network. So, don't be afraid to seek people out and join groups for recovering addicts.

SELF-HARM AND EATING DISORDERS: HOW TO CHANGE THOUGHTS AND BEHAVIOR

Self-harm is the deliberate act of hurting oneself by causing pain or injury. It includes behaviors such as cutting, biting, burning, or scratching at one's skin, hitting oneself, pulling out hair, or repeatedly getting in dangerous situations. It can also involve substance abuse, including deliberately overdosing on medications.

People who engage in self-harm do so in response to intense emotional pain, overwhelming feelings of distress, and painful memories. Many people have described self-harm as a way for them to:

- Express thoughts and feelings that are difficult to put into words.
- Make invisible thoughts and feelings visible to all.
- Turn emotional pain into physical pain.
- Create a feeling of being in control.
- Reduce the intensity of overwhelming thoughts or feelings.

- Detach from traumatic memories.
- Punish themselves for traumatic experiences.
- Stop feeling detached, dissociated, and numb to emotional pain.
- Express suicidal thoughts and feelings without committing suicide.

Individuals who self-harm don't necessarily want to die but may have suicidal ideations. For some, the physical pain caused by injuring themselves offers temporary relief from the overwhelming emotional pain. In this way, they use self-harm as a coping strategy to continue to live.

Even though self-harm provides short-term release, it doesn't remove the source of your distress. Instead, it can bring up some strong emotions and amplify underlying feelings. You may self-harm with no intention of taking your own life, but there is still a risk of accidental death.

Suppose self-harm doesn't offer the brief respite you seek. In that case, you may feel the need to injure yourself more severely or may start to believe that your emotional pain will never end. This can make suicidal ideations stronger.

Self-harm often co-occurs with eating disorders. Both are maladaptive coping strategies for mental distress. They are also dysfunctional in communicating a need for help or support.

For example, suppose you attempted to communicate your needs and were not listened to until you engaged in self-injurious behavior. In that case, it can reinforce the beliefs that it is the only way to get the support you need.

That belief is harmful and ineffective, but it makes sense to the individual self-harming. So, you might continue to engage in that behavior, fearing that you won't receive care or support otherwise.

Many argue that eating disorders are self-harm behaviors. However, eating disorders such as bulimia nervosa, anorexia nervosa, or binge eating typically occur with other psychiatric conditions and disorders.

The motivations behind these disorders are similar to self-harming behaviors. So, it is common for people struggling with an eating disorder to engage in self-harming behaviors, such as cutting simultaneously.

Low self-esteem is one of the biggest underlying causes of self-harm and eating disorders. Self-esteem is defined as "a realistic, appreciative opinion of oneself." In other words, it is accurate, positive, and self-adulatory.

Self-esteem is usually stable, but it may fluctuate depending on thinking patterns influenced by your looks, physical health, relationships, etc.

Individuals with low self-esteem have unrealistic and negative opinions of themselves. They believe they are unworthy of love and respect and below other people. Research has shown that low self-esteem contributes to the following:

- Anxiety and depression
- Stress
- Psychosomatic illness (headache, fatigue, and insomnia)

- Alcohol and drug abuse
- Dependency
- Social challenges
- Unhealthy dieting
- Eating disorders

Self-esteem is directly linked to happiness, optimal mental health, and overall life satisfaction. Individuals with high self-esteem are less troubled by internal problems and mental health issues than those with low self-esteem. Combating self-esteem with cognitive behavioral therapy can help you stop engaging in self-harming behaviors.

CBT for Low Self-Esteem – 5 Key Tools

These five tools can help you build your self-esteem and self-confidence:

Valuing yourself

Low self-esteem may begin in childhood, but it can fluctuate or fall due to traumatic events or life challenges. Think about what you were doing when your self-esteem was higher than it is now. Did you stop doing those things? If so, consider starting them again. Here are some ways to practice valuing yourself:

1. Do things that you genuinely enjoy. This should be anything healthy, such as writing, reading, cooking, gardening, traveling, painting, walking in nature, etc.
2. Recognize your positive traits and strengths.

3. Affirm yourself to improve your sense of personal identity.
4. Challenge limiting beliefs.

Accepting yourself

Self-acceptance means valuing yourself even when you aren't how you think you should be. Know that making mistakes or having flaws doesn't make you worthless.

1. Don't judge yourself for failings or weaknesses.
2. Replace prescriptive statements with preferences. For example, don't say, "I mustn't make another mistake," say "I will try my best not to make another mistake."
3. Embrace your looks.
4. Acknowledge your faults and accept them by reminding yourself that everyone has faults.
5. Challenge your beliefs.

Looking after yourself (self-care)

Taking good care of your body and mind can help you feel your best mentally. Don't ignore your physical or emotional needs or cater to them with a quick fix.

1. Exercise regularly – up to five times a week.
2. Get an appropriate amount of sleep daily.
3. Adopt healthier eating habits. You can switch to a Mediterranean diet.

Understanding yourself

1. Identify underlying personal causes of low self-esteem.
2. Create a more rounded image of yourself, your aspirations, and your values.
3. Confront your fear of what people might think about you.
4. Start a self-esteem journal. Write down personal notes of reflection and express your true feelings and thoughts.

Empowering yourself

Empowering yourself means adopting assertive communication. Be assertive when you express your thoughts, feelings, and needs. Allow others to express themselves constructively.

1. Describe any situation or behavior that is upsetting you clearly and specifically.
2. Try your best to explain how the situation makes you feel.
3. Ask the other person to make reasonable changes that you believe would help.
4. Listen to their perspective and negotiate a solution that works for both parties.

Building your self-esteem takes consistent, intentional effort. Create a plan to implement these steps in your life in the long term.

WHY SELF-CARE IS CRUCIAL

We often overlook self-care, thanks to the number of stressors and responsibilities in life. Despite what you may think, self-care isn't something you practice just for stress, anxiety, depression, OCD, or other mental health issues. You don't have to be struggling with mental health problems to take care of your mind and body.

Self-care doesn't have to be elaborate. It can be as simple as eating healthy, getting enough sleep, exercising, and engaging in fun physical activities. Everyone should take a more active role in protecting their physical and mental well-being – even more so when stressed.

Here are my top ten activities for physical and mental self-care.

- Read a book or magazine for at least an hour. Reading is an excellent way to escape life's many challenges and practice self-care.
- Go outside and walk in nature. Any activity at all is better than none.
- Listen to your favorite artists or any soothing music.
- Get out of bed, shower, and dress your best for no particular reason.
- Declutter your home or workspace.
- Drink water first thing when you wake up, instead of coffee or tea.
- Get some naps regularly.
- Do some yoga.
- Use positive self-affirmations.

- Unplug from social media and technology

Think of more activities you can enjoy and engage in more frequently than you currently do.

Having a great support network makes overcoming addictions and obsessive behavior easier. Asking for help doesn't make you weak or needy. And if you try these techniques on your own without any apparent success, that doesn't make you a failure. These are complex mental health issues, and needing extra help is expected.

Chronic pain requires making a special effort to care for yourself. Thankfully, there are CBT techniques to help you manage pain levels. In the final chapter, I discuss the cause of pain and how CBT can help you change your relationship with pain.

Chapter Eight Highlights

- Obsessive behaviors and addiction are a byproduct of negative thought patterns. Challenge negative thoughts and self-beliefs by writing them in a journal and cross-examining them with objective evidence. Even a 15-minute journaling session every day will make a significant difference.
- Exposure is the fastest way to weaken anxiety's hold over you. Take as little as 30 minutes weekly to expose yourself to situations that trigger your compulsion, and practice ignoring the anxiety until it fades away.

- Mindfulness plays a key role in OCD and addiction treatment. Stay in tune with your emotional state at all times.
- Healthy self-esteem is essential for optimal mental and emotional health. So workout, visit a spa, watch a romantic comedy, and participate in pleasurable activities to nourish your self-esteem with regular self-care.

MANAGING CHRONIC PAIN WITH CBT

P ain is a physical sensation and an emotional experience that is often the result of tissue damage. It alerts the body to react to and prevent further damage. While there is no doubt that pain is real, the brain has a way of amplifying chronic pain and making it seem worse than it is. However, how you view pain, and your relationship with it, can be improved when you adjust your thoughts. In this chapter, we will be looking at CBT techniques for successful pain management.

We all experience pain differently. If I were to ask you to describe pain, your description would vary from mine. That is because there are different ways to feel pain. Unfortunately, this variation in the experience of pain can, in many cases, make it difficult to diagnose, define, or treat it.

Pain ranges from tingling to burning, prickling, stinging, aching, etc. And it can be sharp or full. Additionally, pain is either acute (temporary and brief) or chronic (long-lasting and problematic for your health).

You feel pain when a signal is sent to the brain via nerve fibers for interpretation. More specifically, a group of nerves called "nociceptors" are the body's pain alarm. These nerves detect tissue damage and immediately send words about the damage to the brain, traveling along the spinal cord.

For example, a message is immediately conveyed via a reflex arc in your spine when you unknowingly touch a hot surface. That triggers your muscles to contract, causing you to pull away from the hot surface. Ultimately, the goal is to limit further damage.

The reflex reaction to touching the hot surface occurs before the pain signal reaches the brain. But when it arrives, you feel the unpleasant sensation we all know as pain. Your brain's interpretation of the signal and the efficient operation of the communication channel via which the message is conveyed dictates how you experience pain.

Usually, the brain also releases feel-good neurotransmitters, like dopamine, to counter the unpleasant sensation of pain.

I mentioned that there are two types of pain: Acute and Chronic. Acute pain triggers the fight-or-flight response to alert you to localized tissue damage or an injury. We all experience acute pain every now and then; it is intense and brief. You can get rid of acute pain by treating the underlying injury.

On the other hand, chronic pain is much more intense than acute pain and has no cure. It can be continuous or intermittent, mild or severe. For example, arthritis causes persistent pain, whereas migraine episodes happen intermittently. Intermittent pain happens repeatedly but typically stops between flares.

A key difference between acute and chronic pain is that the latter doesn't trigger the fight-or-flight reaction. At first, it does, but eventually, your sympathetic nervous system adapts to the pain stimulus, causing it to halt the activation of this response system.

Chronic pain is what I want to focus on, so let's delve into the common causes.

COMMON CAUSES OF CHRONIC PAIN

Depending on the cause, the pain has a normal healing time. But once pain lasts over three months or beyond the normal healing time, it becomes chronic. Chronic pain is complex, and it is usually experienced on most days – whether mildly or severely.

Typical pain becomes less severe as the source of injury heals. However, with chronic pain, the body continues to transmit pain signals to the brain. Often, this happens even after the injury behind the pain heals.

Chronic pain may last several weeks, months, or even years. It limits mobility and reduces strength, endurance, and flexibility. It can make it much harder to complete your daily tasks and activities. From experience, it can occur in any body part, but the feeling often differs across the affected areas.

Some common types of chronic pain you should be familiar with are:

- Migraine
- Post-trauma pain
- Post-surgical pain
- Cancer pain
- Lower back pain
- Arthritis
- Neurogenic pain (caused by nerve damage)
- Psychogenic pain (isn't caused by injury, disease, tissue, or nerve damage)

The American Academy of Pain Medicine reports that over 1.5 billion people globally suffer from chronic pain. In addition, it is the number one cause of long-term disability in the U.S., with about 100 million United States citizens affected.

Chronic pain doesn't just happen. Varying factors can cause it. Sometimes, the primary cause may be an initial injury, such as a pulled muscle or a back sprain. Chronic pain is said to develop after nerve damage occurs from the initial injury. That makes the pain more intense and long-lasting. You cannot eliminate chronic pain simply by treating the original underlying injury.

However, there are many cases where chronic pain doesn't have any underlying injury. The specific causes in these cases aren't well understood yet. Often, certain health conditions accompanying aging may cause chronic pain in how they affect the joints and bones.

Some kinds of chronic pain can have multiple causes. For example, lower back pain may be caused by one or more of the factors below:

- Long-term poor posture
- Traumatic injury
- Obesity – which puts strain on the back and knees
- Wearing high heels all the time
- Poor sleeping habit
- Aging of the spinal cord
- Improper lifting of weights or heavy objects
- A congenital physical condition

Chronic pain is sometimes caused by disease. The following diseases and medical conditions may result in the development of long-term pain.

- **Chronic fatigue syndrome:** a condition characterized by prolonged tiredness typically accompanied by pain.
- **Fibromyalgia:** intense, widespread pain across the bones and muscles.
- **Endometriosis is** a disorder where the uterine lining grows outside the uterus, causing severe pain.
- **Inflammatory bowel syndrome:** a set of conditions characterized by chronic inflammation in the digestive tract.
- **Interstitial cystitis:** a disorder marked by pressure and pain in the bladder.

Rheumatoid arthritis, osteoarthritis, cancer, AIDS, multiple sclerosis, gallbladder disease, and stomach ulcers are some other diseases that can cause chronic pain.

Despite all the causes we've identified, the source of chronic pain can be complex and mysterious. Although it may begin with an illness, injury, or any underlying conditions highlighted above, persistent pain can take a psychological turn after the physical cause has healed.

That alone makes it incredibly hard to pinpoint a specific course of treatment and why you are advised to try various curative techniques for chronic pain.

BRAIN MECHANISMS AND PAIN

Without a doubt, chronic pain is every bit as real as it feels, but the cause isn't always what we think it is. For example, when there is tissue damage in the lower back, the brain receives signals.

Chronic pain charges the front area of the brain cortex to run at full throttle. This wears down the neurons, changing synaptic connections in the brain. This continuous neuron firing can cause the brain to develop a dysfunction that feels like lower back pain.

That pain is present, but the source is the brain, not the back. This demonstrates that brain dysfunction is not directly linked with pain sensation in chronic pain patients.

As a result, people with chronic pain rarely only suffer from the physical sensations of burning pain. They also struggle with anxiety, depression, and sleeplessness. Some may even have trouble making the simplest decisions.

Research has established that chronic pain can trigger these pain-related symptoms. In other words, due to the brain mechanisms of chronic pain, there is a real connection between pain, anxiety, and depression.

Everyone has to deal with pain at some point in their lives. Still, for individuals with anxiety or depression, pain is particularly intense and difficult to define or treat. As an example, if you suffer from depression, you're also likely to experience extreme, long-lasting pain compared to other people.

This overlap of pain, anxiety, and depression is particularly highlighted in chronic pain disorders, such as irritable bowel syndrome, fibromyalgia, migraine, nerve pain, and lower back pain. Some psychiatric disorders also contribute to the intensity of pain and an increased risk of disability.

In the past, researchers believed that the relationship between anxiety, depression, and pain was purely a product of psychological factors rather than biological ones. Chronic pain can be depressing, and major depressive disorder likewise causes physical pain sensations.

However, with more advanced research and an increased understanding of how the nervous system interacts with other body systems, it has been established that pain has biological mechanisms similar to anxiety and depression.

Shared anatomy is a major cause of this interconnectedness. The somatosensory cortex, which is the area of the brain responsible for interpreting sensations such as touch, interacts with the hypothalamus, the amygdala, and the anterior cingulate gyrus (parts of the brain in charge of regulating emotions and the stress response) to create the physical and psychological experience of pain. These regions also contribute to the experience of anxiety and depression.

Additionally, serotonin and norepinephrine (both neurotransmitters) contribute to alerting pain signals in the brain and nervous system. They both contribute to anxiety and depression as well.

Chronic pain can be challenging to manage or treat, even more so when it overlaps with anxiety or depression. Sometimes, a clinician may focus on pain, masking the awareness of the presence of a psychiatric condition. But even when both conditions are accurately diagnosed, chronic pain is still difficult to treat.

Living with chronic pain is one of the hardest things to do. It can make it hard to work, care for yourself, and do the things you like. More often than not, chronic pain leads to anxiety or depression. It can also negatively impact your mood and sleep.

Medications aren't the only way to effectively manage or treat chronic pain. If you are on medication for chronic pain, it's best to take a psychological approach to treatment. Individuals with chronic pain who take an active approach to managing their pain daily do better than those who try passive solutions such as medication or surgery.

Cognitive behavioral therapy is one of the best treatment approaches for when pain occurs alone or with anxiety or depression.

HOW CAN CBT HELP THE SYMPTOMS OF CHRONIC PAIN

"It's all in your head."

This is something you've probably heard a few times as someone who suffers from chronic pain – especially when the pain has no apparent cause. But you know the discomfort is real, and you can feel it all too well in your body. So when you're lying in bed, aching and hurting, pain becomes your whole world. Fortunately, that's where cognitive behavioral therapy as an approach to pain management comes in.

As you know, CBT advocates that we create our own experiences, including pain. CBT tells you that pain perception is in the brain, meaning you can affect physical pain by challenging the thoughts and behaviors underlying it. By changing your negative thoughts and attitude toward pain, you can change your awareness of pain and learn better ways to cope, even if the pain intensity never changes.

If you live with chronic pain, what can CBT do for you?

Cognitive behavioral therapy can help you relieve pain in a few ways. First, it changes how you view your pain. With certain CBT techniques, you can change the thoughts, emotions, and behavior related to what you're experiencing and view the discomfort in a much more positive context. You learn that pain doesn't have to interfere with your quality of life, allowing you to function better.

You can also use CBT to change how the brain physically responds to pain. As you know, that is what makes the pain worse. Pain triggers stress, impacting pain control chemicals such as serotonin and norepinephrine.

You can reduce the arousal that affects these brain chemicals using CBT pain management techniques. That, in effect, improves the brain's default pain relief response, making it more powerful than ever.

Combining CBT with other pain management strategies to treat chronic pain would help treat your symptoms. This could be medications, massage, physical therapy, or surgery. Compared to these other remedies, CBT has fewer side effects and risks.

Cognitive behavioral therapy for pain relief encourages you to adopt a problem-solving attitude. One of the worst things about chronic pain is that it induces a sense of helplessness – "I can't do anything about my pain." But if you take action, no matter how little, you will find that it gives you more control and the ability to impact the situation the way you choose.

Perhaps the best thing is that you can do everything necessary yourself. Practicing CBT techniques on your own to control your pain is why CBT is so popular; in fact, self-help CBT sessions are just as effective for treating chronic pain as one-on-one sessions with licensed CBT therapists.

Before you begin pain management with CBT, you should talk with your doctor first. You need a professional to assess your level of pain, as well as the history and current pain management remedies. Your doctor may refer you to a cognitive behavioral therapist to conduct a general psychological assessment to identify underlying issues that may worsen the pain.

Whether you see a professional first or not, you can still start a CBT pain management program. You only need individual sessions for at least 45 minutes and up to two hours weekly. However, you might need between 8 and 24 sessions to achieve your pain control goal.

Before you begin, here's how you can get the most out of the process.

- First, you have to believe it will work. Some people take a cautious approach to CBT because they think, "How will it work?" If you don't believe it'll work, you won't participate in the process as you should or do well.
- You have to engage with the techniques actively. As with most things, you get what you put into the process. The more work you put into sessions and assignments, the better your pain management outcome will be.
- Practice all recommended skills. Engage with new ways of thinking and acting in response to pain, even when you aren't in pain. You should keep a log of your pain and the specific skills that work in your fight against it. The more you practice, the easier it will be to draw on your skills when needed.

- Keeping an open mind is essential. You have to accept that an alternative way of viewing things may be more helpful for you. CBT may not work for pain relief if you have difficulty taking a different approach

The Chronic Pain Cycle

Many factors contribute to pain and fatigue, on top of whatever condition is underlying the pain. Due to the fatigue caused by persistent, chronic pain, it's easy to fall into a pattern of inactivity and rest that is, unfortunately, not the best way to deal with pain. Therefore, breaking this seemingly harmless cycle is important by stopping before the pain or fatigue forces you to stop.

An example is resting too much for too long. The more you rest, the more symptoms will develop. In addition, prolonged rest after an injury or illness can make it harder to become active once again, thus increasing fatigue. Also, it negatively affects the heart, lungs, muscles, and nervous system.

Doing too much too soon after an injury or illness because you have some energy can also contribute to pain and fatigue. It can make you feel more tired and put you in even more pain, forcing you into prolonged rest.

Fixating on pain and fatigue is another way to complicate chronic pain. Worrying about your pain makes it more prominent in your thoughts. That can affect your emotions, resulting in fatigue and even more pain. If you worry that your symptoms mean the pain is worsening, especially after physical activity, you might worry that you're harming yourself by becoming active again.

These can make you feel low, frustrated, anxious, helpless, and even depressed. In turn, this can make you feel more tired and in pain. These are all psychological factors that interact with each other, so it's like having multiple double-ended arrows pointed at you while stuck in a circle.

PACING YOURSELF

As someone who suffers from chronic pain and fatigue, you know how difficult it can be to complete tasks when you're having a flare-up, i.e., an episode of severe pain. As a result, you may feel the urge to push yourself too hard or avoid tasks altogether. Unfortunately, this creates a "boom or bust" pattern of activity.

"Boom" is used for days when you're bustling with energy and overactive, whereas "Bust" is when you're tired and underactive.

Pacing yourself, which means taking a break before the pain forces you to, is a technique to limit the interference of pain flares in your daily life. It is specifically for people who cannot effectively manage their pain and fatigue. It helps you manage the "boom or bust" pattern to find a balance.

The framework for pacing yourself includes the following:

- Recognizing unhelpful behavioral patterns
- Finding baselines

- Learning to exercise self-compassion
- Being flexible
- Gradually increase your progress in different activities

It's important to embrace flexibility rather than rigidity when thinking about the things you need to get done.

Some key components of pacing yourself include:

- Breaking down your tasks into smaller, more manageable ones.
- Be kind to yourself.
- Saying 'no'
- Creating a structure or routine.
- Using every lunch or rest break

It's possible to experience "boom and bust" if you do too much in a day, even if you feel energized and okay. For example, if you're suffering from chronic pain due to fibromyalgia, you may want to clean the house and do some stuff here and there because you don't feel as much pain and have some energy. But you may have to pay for that for the rest of the week.

Learning to pace yourself can be difficult. You may feel like it takes longer to complete some tasks or activities, even though it isn't the case. For example, it will take less effort to plan to do some gardening over two days compared to exerting yourself to complete it one day and dealing with increased pain and fatigue throughout the following week.

It would be best if you devised a pacing strategy that works well for you when working independently. Here are the steps to pace yourself effectively:

- **Calculate your baselines**

Your baseline is how long it takes to perform a task without worsening your symptoms. When you have an activity, set a timer for your baseline. For example, if standing for 25 minutes flares up your pain and makes you tired, your standing baseline should be 15 minutes.

Note: Time isn't always the measure of pacing. For activities such as exercises, you can use repetitions as a measure. Set your baseline according to a "bust" when you can still do an activity, no matter how little.

- **Structure your day**

There is a traffic light system to help you structure your day and practice better pacing. Use this to create a table of your daily activities for every day of the week and mark each activity with the right color. For example, red = demanding; amber = moderate; and green = relaxing. It will help you structure and improve your day.

Below is an example of what your table should look like.

	Mon	Tues	Weds	Thurs	Fri	Sat	Sun
7-8 am	Breakfast	Breakfast	Breakfast	Breakfast	Breakfast	Sleep	Sleep
8-9 am	Get ready	Get ready	Get ready	Get ready	Get ready	Sleep	Sleep
9-10 am	Work	Work	Work	Work	Outdoors	Sleep	Sleep
10-11 am	Work	Work	Work	Work	Shopping	Breakfast	Breakfast

You can fill the table in to include activities that you do every day.

- **Plan your week**

Think of ways to classify the long periods of red activity by mixing in some green or amber activity. For example, if certain tasks must be completed at specific times, highlight them with appropriate colors. Also, break tasks into smaller ones according to priority.

Once you've established and stabilized a routine, you can start pacing up to increase daily activity. Again, choose a realistic baseline buildup rate and allow your body to adapt before climbing. Most importantly, make the increases gradual, steady, and routine.

QUESTIONING THOUGHTS REGARDING PAIN

I know what you're thinking – that I want you to question if your pain is real. This is inaccurate. Questioning thoughts regarding pain isn't about challenging the realness of your pain. Rather, it's about challenging your negative views of pain. Negative thoughts contribute to worsening pain and fatigue symptoms more than you know.

Living with chronic pain often means struggling with overwhelming negative thoughts and feelings — pain catastrophizing. The mere sound of "catastrophizing" can make this concept seem judgmental, but it's just negative thinking.

Pain catastrophizing is when you have persistent negative thoughts and feelings related to chronic pain, which interfere with daily functioning. Negative thinking patterns related to chronic pain arise from the 3 "I"s of pain – infinite, insurmountable, and incurable. All refer to our perception of pain.

You have to understand that the experience of pain is more layered than how we physically perceive it. Negative thinking related to pain affects self-efficacy and the ability to function normally in social situations.

Negative thinking may be impacting your quality of life in these three ways:

- Magnification – magnifying your pain and the possibility of it getting worse.
- Rumination – constantly thinking about your pain to the point where it distracts you from other things.

- Helplessness – losing hope in your ability to overcome your pain.

Some negative thoughts associated with chronic pain include:

- *"My pain will never end. I'm stuck with it for the rest of my life."*
- *"I can't keep my pain out of my mind."*
- *"It hurts so bad. I don't think it will ever stop."*
- *"Something serious is bound to happen to me."*

Positive Self-Talk is a great CBT technique to challenge negative thoughts related to pain. The idea is to slow the waterfall of negative thoughts before they send you over the falls. You can use positive self-talk to replace the narrative building about yourself inside your head.

We've covered positive self-talk (affirmations) extensively. Nevertheless, here are three positive affirmations regarding pain to get started.

- *"I am learning to change my pain."*
- *"I might still have some level of pain, but I am making great progress, and I'm proud of how far I have come."*
- *"My pain may not be gone, but I am becoming more resilient and dealing with it better."*

Another technique to challenge pain-related thoughts is "Moving with your mind." It is effective for anyone struggling with lower back pain, rheumatoid arthritis, fibromyalgia, etc.

As you pace and slowly rebuild your strength, it's normal for your mind to get anxious. Anxiety is meant to protect you from potential danger.

So, your mind resorts to constantly showing you the worst-case scenario or highlighting potential *doom and gloom* situations.

Try this exercise:

- Notice any negative thought that arises with the activity you're trying to do.
- Label the negative thought.
- Do the activity anyway.

It may look like this:

- *"I shouldn't walk because what if I fall and hurt my knees some more? Walking isn't good for me."*
- *"No! This is a negative story created to stop me."*

Start walking and see if the thought subsides.

You may be surprised at how quickly you can change your thoughts or make them subside. These techniques can make negative thoughts go away or dissolute into unrelated thoughts. You can improve your self-confidence and decrease pain-related anxiety and depression. CBT offers a simple way to overcome pain and live your life to the fullest.

BODY SCANNING: GUIDED MEDITATION FOR PAIN RELIEF

Do this body scanning exercise for 45 minutes every day.

- Lie down comfortably on a flat surface. You may use your bed or a meditation mat.
- Shut your eyes and focus on your breath.
- Inhale and exhale deeply. As you breathe in and out, notice the rise and fall of your belly.
- Focus on your left foot. Pay attention to how you feel and if there's any pain in that part of your body. Continue to breathe in and out gently.
- Keep the attention on your foot. Even as your thoughts come and go, keep focusing on the foot.
- Notice any pain and what you're feeling at the moment. Observe the pain; don't judge or try to alleviate it.
- Slowly pull your attention away from your left foot and bring it to your left ankle. This is scanning.
- Continue scanning and work up, repeating the steps above.

Regular meditation can positively impact all aspects of your physical and mental well-being. It can help you reduce stress, improve focus, and cope better with chronic pain.

Chapter Nine Highlights

- CBT for chronic pain focuses on changing thought and behavioral patterns to address the problematic thoughts-feelings-behaviors cycle contributing to pain. CBT techniques may not eliminate pain entirely, but they can help you change your thoughts and behaviors to increase tolerance and decrease pain intensity.
- Pain often presents with other psychological problems such as anxiety, depression, borderline personality disorder, etc. CBT can treat all possible underlying mental health problems while treating chronic pain.
- Chronic pain often leads to fatigue, creating a cycle where being in pain makes you tired, and being tired puts you in further discomfort. Pacing is a CBT pain management method that can help you break free of this cycle.
- Cognitive reframing can change your perception of pain, thus positively influencing how you respond to it.

CONCLUSION

Wow! It's been such an exciting journey with you, and I am glad you made it to the end. I believe you've now gained invaluable skills you can use to live a peaceful and fulfilling life. But before I go, let me leave you with a few words.

Like me, I want everyone suffering from the effect of distorted thoughts to benefit from CBT skills and techniques. When you use the skills discussed in this book, you can now deal with the issues you're presently facing due to unhelpful thought patterns.

So far, you've learned what CBT entails and how to help yourself with it. You've discovered where thoughts come from and the connection between your thoughts, emotions, and actions. By examining cognitive distortions, you can easily identify and become aware of them when it happens.

We discussed learning how to rewire your brain and over-coming negative thoughts. When you know this, it will be easier to change your emotions by addressing your cognition and behavior.

You've learned how to use CBT to address OCD, anxiety, chronic pain, and panic attacks due to negative thoughts. When you know more about your triggers and emotional regulation, you can take control of anxiety and depression.

As you navigate life, don't give up on the hard work you've dedicated to this journey. Even if you find yourself slipping, re-strategize and keep on moving. I encourage you to always approach what you've learned positively. Allowing negativity means you're setting the stage rolling for failure, and that isn't what we want. So, approach any issue you may face with an open mind. Put in the effort, and you'll see that the result will be worth it.

As I end this journey, I'd appreciate it if you could take a few seconds to help someone by dropping a review and mentioning how this book has been helpful.

See you on the positive side of life!

REFERENCES

Ackerman, C.E. (n.d). *CBT Techniques: 25 Cognitive Behavioral Therapy Worksheets.* Retrieved from https://positivepsychology.com/cbt-cognitive-behavioral-therapy-techniques-worksheets/#cbt-tools

Ackerman, C.E. (n.d). *CBT's Cognitive Restructuring (CR) For Tackling Cognitive Distortions.* Retrieved from https://positivepsychology.com/cbt-cognitive-restructuring-cognitive-distortions/

Ackerman, C.E. (n.d). *What Is Neuroplasticity? A Psychologist Explains [+14 Tools].* Retrieved from https://positivepsychology.com/neuroplasticity/

Action News. (July, 2021). *Best Life: Practice these tips to stay calm during a panic attack.* Retrieved from https://www.actionnews5.com/2021/07/16/best-life-practice-these-tips-stay-calm-during-panic-attack/

American Psychological Association (n.d.) *Different approaches to psychotherapy.* Retrieved from https://www.apa.org/topics/psychotherapy/approaches

American Psychological Association (n.d.) *What Is Cognitive Behavioral Therapy?* Retrieved from https://www.apa.org/ptsd-guideline/patients-and-families/cognitive-behavioral

Anxiety Canada. (n.d). Tool 4: *Resisting the Quick Fix.* Retrieved from Tool 4: Resisting the Quick Fix - Anxiety Canada

Barrell, A. (April, 2020). *Stress vs. anxiety: How to tell the difference.* Retrieved from https://www.medicalnewstoday.com/articles/stress-vs-anxiety

Begdache, L. (March, 2019). *Ask a Scientist: Neurons help explain how our brains think.* Retrieved from https://www.pressconnects.com/story/news/local/2019/03/18/ask-scientist-how-do-thoughts-work-our-brain/3153303002/

Better Health. (n.d). *Panic attack.* Retrieved from https://www.betterhealth.vic.gov.au/health/conditionsandtreatments/panic-attack

Bjarnadottir, A. (June, 2019). *Mindful Eating 101 — A Beginner's Guide.* Retrieved from https://www.healthline.com/nutrition/mindful-eating-guide

Bravely She Blogs. (November, 2019). *How To Challenge Negative Automatic Thoughts When You Are Depressed.* Retrieved from https://www.bravelyshe blogs.com/how-to-deal-with-automatic-negative-thoughts-ants-when-

you-are-depressed/
#Always_remember_depression_does_not_define_you_Y
ou_are_stronger_than_you_think_you_are_and_every_step_you_
take_in_this_journey_reflects_your_true_strength

Bowers, S. (June, 2011). *Managing Chronic Pain: A Cognitive-Behavioral Therapy Approach.* Retrieved from https://www.webmd.com/pain-management/features/cognitive-behavioral

Butler, S. (n.d). *Are You Stuck in Fight or Flight?* Retrieved from https://www.thejoint.com/florida/orlando/town-park-27010/202407-are-you-stuck-in-fight-flight

Calzadilla, S. (March, 2022). *41 Journal Prompts for Depression.* Retrieved from https://www.choosingtherapy.com/journal-prompts-for-depression/

Carpenter, J. K., Andrews, L. A., Witcraft, S. M., Powers, M. B., Smits, J., & Hofmann, S. G. (2018). *Cognitive Behavioral Therapy For Anxiety And Related Disorders: A Meta-Analysis Of Randomized Placebo-Controlled Trials.* Retrieved from https://doi.org/10.1002/da.22728

CBT Los Angeles (n.d). *Does CBT Work?* Retrieved from https://cogbtherapy.-com/how-effective-is-cbt-compared-to-other-treatments

Cherry, K. ((August, 2022). *What Is Cognitive Behavioral Therapy (CBT)?* Retrieved from https://www.verywellmind.com/what-is-cognitive-behavior-therapy-2795747

Clack-Jones, T. (June, 2014). *Stress less with mindful walking.* Retrieved from https://www.canr.msu.edu/news/stress_less_with_mindful_walking

Cleveland Clinic. (n.d). *Diaphragmatic Breathing.* Retrieved from https://my.clevelandclinic.org/health/articles/9445-diaphragmatic-breathing

Cognitive Behavioral Therapy Los Angeles. (n.d). *Does CBT Work?* Retrieved from https://cogbtherapy.com/how-effective-is-cbt-compared-to-other-treatments

Cooper, M. (n.d). *7 Ways to Face Down Your Fear of Failure and Come Out Stronger on the Other Side.* Retrieved from 7 Ways to Get Over Your Fear of Failure | The Muse

Cronkleton, E. (April, 2019). *10 Breathing Techniques for Stress Relief and More.* Retrieved from https://www.healthline.com/health/breathing-exercise

Davies, M. N., Verdi, S., Burri, A., Trzaskowski, M., Lee, M., Hettema, J. M., Jansen, R., Boomsma, D. I., & Spector, T. D. (2015). *Generalised Anxiety Disorder--A Twin Study of Genetic Architecture, Genome-Wide Association and*

Differential Gene Expression. Retrieved from https://doi.org/10.1371/jour nal.pone.0134865

Department Of Health Republic Of The Philippines. (n.d). *Patient's Workbook For Cognitive Behavioral Therapy Sessions.* Retrieved from https://www.jica. go.jp/project/philippines/013/materials/ku57pq00003ud3mz-att/ material_02a.pdf

Domschke, K., & Maron, E. (2013). *Genetic factors in anxiety disorders.* Retrieved from https://doi.org/10.1159/000351932

Lanese, N. & Dutfield, S. (February, 2022). *Fight or flight: The sympathetic nervous system.* Retrieved from https://www.livescience.com/65446-sympathetic-nervous-system.html

Ellis, M. (June, 2020). *How to Cope With Crippling Anxiety and Knowing When to Seek Treatment.* Retrieved from How to Cope With Crippling Anxiety and Knowing When to Seek Treatment – Bridges to Recovery

Fenn, K & Byrne, M. (September, 2013). *The Key Principles Of Cognitive Behavioural Therapy.* Retrieved from https://journals.sagepub.-com/doi/10.1177/1755738012471029

Felman, A. (February, 2022). *What is pain, and how do you treat it?* Retrieved from https://www.medicalnewstoday.com/articles/145750

Fitzgerald, S. (2017). *The CBT Workbook: Change Your Life With Cognitive Behavioral Therapy.* John Murray Learning , Camelite House.

Forhims.com. (February, 2021). *Anxiety Triggers: How to Identify & Overcome Them.* Retrieved from https://www.forhims.com/blog/common-anxiety-triggers

Gillihan, S. (2006) *Retrain Your Brain: Cognitive Behavioral Therapy In 7 Weeks.* Althea Press.

Good Therapy. (n.d). *Self-Criticism.* Retrieved from Therapy for Self Criticism, Therapist for Self Criticism (goodtherapy.org)

Groff & Associates. (n.d). *5 Easy Steps to Changing Your Thinking Using Cognitive Behavioral Therapy (CBT).* Retrieved from https://groffandassociates.com/ 2017/10/12/5-easy-steps-to-changing-your-thinking-using-cognitive-behavioral-therapy-cbt/

Ground Work Counseling. (n.d). *Anxiety and Criticism* – How CBT Can Help You Overcome Your Anxiety. Retrieved from Anxiety and Criticism – How CBT Can Help You Overcome Your Anxiety | GroundWork Counseling

Harvard Health Publishing School. (January, 2022). *What causes depression?*

Retrieved from https://www.health.harvard.edu/mind-and-mood/what-causes-depression

Heads Space. (n.d). *Meditation for stress.* Retrieved from https://www.headspace.com/meditation/stress

Heads Up Guys. (n.d). *18 Male Athletes And Celebrities Who've Talked About The Value Of Therapy.* Retrieved from https://headsupguys.org/18-male-athletes-celebrities-whove-talked-value-therapy/

Health Direct. (n.d). *Chronic Pain.* Retrieved from https://www.healthdirect.gov.au/chronic-pain

Ineffable Living. (September, 2022). *Top 18 Self Esteem Exercises (+FREE CBT For Self-Esteem Worksheets PDF).* Retrieved from https://ineffableliving.com/raising-low-self-esteem/#3-cbt-for-low-self-esteem-%E2%80%93-5-key-ingredients-

Jovanovic, T. (n.d). *What Is Anxiety?* Retrieved from https://www.anxiety.org/what-is-anxiety

Kaczkurkin, A. N., & Foa, E. B. (2015). *Cognitive-behavioral therapy for anxiety disorders: an update on the empirical evidence. Dialogues in clinical neuroscience.* Retrieved from https://doi.org/10.31887/DCNS.2015.17.3/akaczkurkin

Kasper S. (2006). *Anxiety disorders: under-diagnosed and insufficiently treated.* International journal of psychiatry in clinical practice, 10 Suppl 1, 3–9. Retrieved from https://doi.org/10.1080/13651500600552297

Keelan, P. (n.d). *A common misconception about cognitive behavioural therapy: It's just about positive thinking.* Retrieved from https://drpatrickkeelan.com/psychology/a-common-misconception-about-cognitive-behavioural-therapy-its-just-about-positive-thinking/

Lee, W. E. et al. (2006). *The Protective Role Of Trait Anxiety: A Longitudinal Cohort Study.* Retrieved from https://www.cambridge.org/core/journals/psychological-medicine/article/abs/protective-role-of-trait-anxiety-a-longitudinal-cohort-study/919A2F6F0C52E512A5F67E3AFE7B7A0F

Let's Talk CBT. (February, 2020). *CBT for Self-Harm.* Retrieved from https://letstalkaboutcbt.libsyn.com/cbt-for-self-harm

Lim, C. (n.d). *This Is Why You Should Be Proud of Making Mistakes.* Retrieved from This Is Why You Should Be Proud Of Making Mistakes (lifehack.org)

Lyle, L. (n.d). *When You Can't Think Away Your Anxious Thoughts, Do This Instead.* Retrieved from When You Can't Think Away Your Anxious Thoughts, Do This Instead (happify.com)

Mayo Clinic (n.d). *Stress symptoms: Effects on your body and behavior.* Retrieved from https://www.mayoclinic.org/healthy-lifestyle/stress-management/in-depth/stress-symptoms/art-20050987

Micah, Abraham. (October, 2020). *How to Perform Exposure Therapy for Anxiety at Home*. Retrieved from https://www.calmclinic.com/anxiety/treatment/exposure-therapy

Mindful.Org. (n.d). *How to Manage Stress with Mindfulness and Meditation*. Retrieved from https://www.mindful.org/how-to-manage-stress-with-mindfulness-and-meditation/#mindfulness

Mind My Peelings. (n.d). *How Cognitive Distortions Creates an Irrational Perception of Reality*. Retrieved from https://www.mindmypeelings.com/blog/cognitive-distortions

Mind Your Mind. (February, 2020). *7 Eating Disorder Recovery Strategies*. Retrieved from https://mindyourmind.ca/blog/7-eating-disorder-recovery-strategies

Mistry, M. (n.d). *7 Signs Your Mistakes Have Made You Stronger Even Though You Don't Feel So*. Retrieved from 7 Signs Your Mistakes Have Made You Stronger Even Though You Don't Feel So - Lifehack

Nawaz, S. (January, 2020). *How Anxiety Traps Us, and How We Can Break Free*. Retrieved from How Anxiety Traps Us, and How We Can Break Free (hbr.org)

NHS Inform. (n.d). *How to deal with panic attacks*. Retrieved from https://www.nhsinform.scot/healthy-living/mental-wellbeing/anxiety-and-panic/how-to-deal-with-panic-attacks

Northwestern University. (February, 2008). *Chronic Pain Harms The Brain*. ScienceDaily. Retrieved December 1, 2022 from www.sciencedaily.com/releases/2008/02/080205171755.htm

Oxford CB UK. (November, 2018). *16 Things To Do For Self-Care*. Retrieved from https://www.oxfordcbt.co.uk/self-care/

Pietrangelo, A. (December, 2019). *9 CBT Techniques for Better Mental Health*. Retrieved from CBT Techniques: Tools for Cognitive Behavioral Therapy (healthline.com)

Pogosyan, M (February, 2021). *Positive Psychology in Therapy: What is Positive CBT?* Retrieved from https://www.psychologytoday.com/intl/blog/between-cultures/202102/positive-psychology-in-therapy-what-is-positive-cbt

Priory Group. (n.d). *How are CBT and mindfulness used to treat OCD?* Retrieved from https://www.priorygroup.com/blog/how-are-cbt-and-mindfulness-used-to-treat-ocd

Psychology Today (n.d) *Cognitive Behavioral Therapy*. Retrieved from https://www.psychologytoday.com/us/basics/cognitive-behavioral-therapy#the-origins-of-cbt

Cassabianca, S. & Shatzman, C. (April, 2022). *46 Positive Affirmations for Anxiety Relief*. Retrieved from https://psychcentral.com/anxiety/affirmations-for-anxiety

NHS. (n.d). *Practical Pacing and Fatigue Management*. Retrieved from https://www.ehlers-danlos.com/wp-content/uploads/Parry-Practical-Pacing-and-Fatigue-Management-S.pdf

Quintero, S. (n.d). *Toxic Positivity: The Dark Side of Positive Vibes*. Retrieved from https://thepsychologygroup.com/toxic-positivity/

RBS Rehab. (n.d). *Cognitive Behavioral Therapy Exercises for Addiction*. Retrieved from https://rbsrehab.com/cognitive-behavioral-therapy-exercises/

Roncero, A. (June, 2021). *Automatic negative thoughts: how to identify and fix them*. Retrieved from https://www.betterup.com/blog/automatic-thoughts

Saxena, S. (Dcember, 2021). *Avoidance Behavior: Examples, Impacts, & How to Overcome*. Retrieved from How to Spot & Overcome Avoidance Behavior (choosingtherapy.com)

Shah, N. (n.d). *Relationship between thoughts, emotions and behaviours – Complete guide*. Retrieved from https://www.visitmhp.com/mental-health/relationship-between-thoughts-emotions-behaviours/

Smith, J. (September, 2020). *How can you stop a panic attack?* Retrieved from https://www.medicalnewstoday.com/articles/321510

Stoppler, M.C. (January, 2022). *Progressive Muscle Relaxation for Stress and Insomnia*. Retrieved from https://www.webmd.com/sleep-disorders/muscle-relaxation-for-stress-insomnia

Tartakovsky, M. (August, 2015). *5 Ways to Expand All-or-Nothing Thinking*. Retrieved from https://psychcentral.com/blog/5-ways-to-expand-all-or-nothing-thinking#1

Teachman, B. (May, 2020). *Why Anxiety Should Not Be Feared*. Retrieved from Why Anxiety Should Not Be Feared | Anxiety and Depression Association of America, ADAA

The OCD and Anxiety Center. (March, 2021). *Rumination*. Retrieved from https://theocdandanxietycenter.com/rumination/

Tyrell, M. (n.d) *15 Core CBT Techniques You Can Use Right Now*. Retrieved from https://www.unk.com/blog/15-core-cbt-techniques-you-can-use-right-now/

Youthful Dynamics. (n.d). It's Exhausting. 16 Quotes Illustrating Life with Anxiety. Retrieved from https://www.youthdynamics.org/its-exhausting-16-quotes-illustrating-life-with-anxiety/